D0044420

ADAM SMITH

Architects of Freedom Series

ADAM SMITH

BY

E. G. WEST

ARLINGTON HOUSE   *New Rochelle, N.Y.*

Prefatory Note

Of the features which make any man worthy of biography the three most important are first his originality, second his ability to mirror his age, and third his own personal drama. While convention has it that biography as such should concentrate upon the last of these, the present work focuses upon all three. This is not merely because of the scantiness of personal biographical material, but also because of the awareness that a triple study of the man, his writings, and his era provides, in Smith's case, a particularly fruitful interaction and reciprocal effect.

Adam Smith's political economy, as we shall endeavor to show, has meaning for all times, and indeed in many ways even the modern era has not yet caught up with it. His personal life, on the other hand, provides an unusually fascinating vignette of that "other world," the eighteenth century. To read it is to open new windows on the illustrious society of pre-revolutionary Europe. How intriguing it is to remember, for instance, that it was Adam Smith who, as a Scottish Professor, taught literary style to Boswell himself. Indeed, as a subject for the pen of that Prince of Biographers, Smith would have proved most worthy. For here, after all, was a man who had spoken with the great Voltaire and had probably met Rousseau; a man who was just as much a clubman as Johnson; a man who not only gave advice to governments but had his advice acted upon; and last but not least, a man of warm human feelings and artless idiosyncrasy. But Smith would never have consented to being studiously chronicled during his lifetime. Indeed, the great man took care to leave behind as little material on his personal life as he could. Fortunately, however, Smith's voluminous writings enable us to accumulate much circumstantial and other evidence on which to build a picture; and when this is correlated with the few biographical details, there is much scope for interesting permutation. The sources of biographical information upon which this volume relies, and references to subsequent studies of most aspects of Smith's work, will be found in the Bibliography at the end of the book.

I wish to record my special thanks to Mrs. Carole Phillips of the University of Kent for so patiently and efficiently typing the manuscript.

Edwin G. West

The University of Kent
Canterbury
England
March, 1969

Contents

ADAM SMITH

CHAPTER I

Adam Smith's Revolution

IT is easy to predict that in the year 1976 the American
people will be making some fitting bicentenary tribute to
Thomas Jefferson, author of the 1776 Declaration of Independence. In Scotland the question of whom to commemo-
rate is well beyond any conjecture. Scotsmen are already well
ahead with arrangements which will do full honor to their
own Adam Smith, who added Scottish glory to the year 1776
with the publication of his celebrated economic treatise, *The
Wealth of Nations.* In many ways Adam Smith belongs to
America as much as does Jefferson. Out of a six-scholar ad-
visory panel now working on the Smith bicentenary committee of the University of Glasgow, three are residents of the
United States. Their membership well symbolizes the enthusiasm with which Smith's original message has been received across the Atlantic. Jefferson and Smith, of course,
complemented each other in their work. Both men, for instance, shared the republican instinct; both argued strongly
for liberty; and Jefferson's plea for political liberty was well
accompanied by Smith's campaign for freedom to trade. For,
in the words of two present-day incumbents of Jefferson's

own University of Virginia, Professors J. M. Buchanan and
Gordon Tullock: "Constitutional democracy in its modern
sense was born as a twin of the market economy."

Of the two champions in the common cause, Adam Smith
has received the less general publicity. While both were distinguished men of letters, Jefferson was also a "man of action," prominent especially in politics and law. Adam Smith's
influence, though taking longer to register, was nevertheless
ultimately just as far-reaching. Twenty years after Smith's
death in 1790, Alexander von der Marwitz, a German student, wrote to a friend about the author of *The Wealth of
Nations:* "Next to Napoleon he is now the mightiest monarch in Europe." Pitt and Shelburne, in their advocacy of
free trade, both declared themselves disciples of Smith. Indeed, Pitt's commercial policy from 1784 to 1794 was ex-
plicitly based on Smithian principles. The commercial treaty
with France, the reduction of debt, customs reform and resolute retrenchment in public expenditure, all of which occurred within a few years of 1776, were all clearly connected
with the great book published in that year.

It was not only the American and French political revolutions, but also the revolution in commercial and economic
thinking which put an end to the remnants of medieval society. Smith's contribution to this thinking was decisive. His
treatise of 1776 struck a mighty blow at the trade walls which
had been erected around the nation states of Europe by the
traditional protectionist or mercantilist politicians. In particular, the belief of many of the latter that one nation could
become richer only if a rival became poorer was subjected to
an especially devastating assault. In Chapter III of Book IV
of his *The Wealth of Nations* Adam Smith remonstrated:

The modern maxims of foreign commerce, by aim-
ing at the impoverishment of all our neighbours,
so far as they are capable of producing their intended effect, tend to render that very commerce
insignificant and contemptible. . . .

A nation that would enrich itself by foreign trade,
is certainly most likely to do so when its neighbours are all rich, industrious, and commercial nations. A great nation surrounded on all sides by
wandering savages and poor barbarians might, no
doubt, acquire riches by the cultivation of its own
lands, and by its own interior commerce, but not
by foreign trade.

Smith ridiculed in particular the artificial barriers against
trade between the two neighboring rich countries of France
and England. Such restrictions, argued Smith, were the outcome of a quiet, domestic conspiracy between self-seeking
tradesmen and politicians. He was the first to concede that
the pursuit of self-interest was not intrinsically bad; what was
needed was a system in which self-interest would be so har-
nessed that it would be an ally and not an enemy of social
prosperity. In general, the private free market mechanism
provided such a system. By pursuing his own interest the
individual frequently promoted that of the society "more
effectually than when he really intends to promote it." But
this result could only occur when the market was free, open
and truly competitive. The argument of protectionist traders
that restrictions on imports would promote "society's interest" was hypocritical. "I have never known much good done
by those who affected to trade for the public good."

The excessive restrictions on trade between England and
France had led to the diversion of trade to the more distant
colonies of the two countries. Smith denounced the futility of

this development in words which have uncanny relevance to the British struggle to enter the European Common Market nearly two centuries later:

> If those two countries, however, were to consider their real interest, without either mercantile jealousy or national animosity, the commerce of France might be more advantageous to Great Britain than that of any other country, and for the same reason that of Great Britain to France.
>
> . . . But the very same circumstances which would have rendered an open and free commerce between the two countries so advantageous to both, have occasioned the principal obstructions to that commerce. Being neighbours, they are necessarily enemies, and the wealth and power of each becomes, upon that account, more formidable to the other; and what would increase the advantage of national friendship, serves only to inflame the violence of national animosity.[1]

Down to Adam Smith's time in the eighteenth century the occupations of commerce and trade were suspect. The activities of buying and selling and lending money were inhibited by the vague feeling that they were sinful. It was felt by some that of two parties to a bargain, the gains of one would somehow be offset by the losses of the other; this was believed to be especially true where the two parties were great nations. The most important consequence of Adam Smith's writings was to shatter these notions. In Smith's "condition of natural liberty," exchange relationships are entered into freely and voluntarily by both parties; the outcome must therefore be *mutually* acceptable. No one individual would *freely* enter into such a relationship knowing that he would come out of it worse off than he started. Thus, in their book, the *Calculus of Consent*, which was the outcome of recent work done at the Thomas Jefferson Center for Studies in Political Economy at the University of Virginia, Professors Buchanan and Tullock emphasize the same point:

> . . . the simple fact is, of course, that in normal trade *all* parties gain; there exist *mutual gains from trade*. The great contribution of Adam Smith lay in his popularization of this simple point. . . . (p. 250)

Adam Smith seems to have been fully aware of the difficulties of devising a suitable political framework wherein the beneficial operations of the free market could best operate. This problem, to which Buchanan and Tullock devoted their book, can readily be recognized the moment we remember that the play of individual self-interest can take place not only in the market place but also at the ballot box and in the political process. These two separate stages of activity give rise to conflict and inconsistency. Acting in their capacity as *consumers* who accept one product and reject another, individuals constitute a potent though dispersed force making for market efficiency. However, in their capacity of *producers*, individuals often recognize that, in majority-voting democracies, their self-interest is more effectively promoted by political lobbying to secure special protection and privileges for their particular occupation or trade. Thus, although as Adam Smith said, "The sole end of economic activity should be consumption," in practice, because of the particular political framework, the interests of producers often predominate. Hence the following rather pessimistic conclusion of Adam Smith:

> To expect, indeed, that the freedom of trade should ever be entirely restored in Great Britain, is as absurd as to expect that an Oceana or Utopia should ever be established in it. Not only the prejudices of the public, but what is much more unconquerable, the private interests of many individuals, irresistibly oppose it.

With sentiments like these, Smith would have been surprised at the extent of the triumph of free trade policies over the next century. He underestimated the power of his own influence and that of other economists to come. Disciples and admirers emerged everywhere. Developing the Scottish professor's arguments and presenting them with his own particularly devastating kind of wit, the French economist Bastiat, for instance, made a telling onslaught upon entrenched monopoly positions in France. In the development of economics during the first half of the nineteenth century, Smith's work was the common point of departure for most professionals and academics. In politics, undoubtedly the crowning triumph came with Sir Robert Peel's overthrow of the Corn Laws, those notorious symbols of protectionism, in the year 1846. By 1850 Disraeli was confident that "protection is not only dead, but damned."

While it can fairly be claimed that Smith's treatise both shocked and instructed his fellow men in the late eighteenth century, it can also be argued that the times were ripe for such a work. The first edition was exhausted in six months. Such a reception came as a surprise both to his publishers and to his friends. Smith's best friend, David Hume, comparing *The Wealth of Nations* with *The Decline and Fall of the Roman Empire* by Edward Gibbon, which had been launched by the same publisher in that same year, remarked:

"The former [Gibbon's work] is the most popular work; but the sale of the latter, though not near so rapid, has been more than I could have expected from a work that requires so much thought and reflection (qualities that do not abound among modern readers) to peruse to any purpose." Five editions of Smith's book appeared between 1776 and 1786. Another five, four English and one Irish, appeared between 1791 and 1799. By the end of the century several editions had appeared in France, Germany, Italy, Spain and other European countries.

But while the timing of the publication of his work was fortunate, we must not neglect to give due credit to its particular internal qualities. Leaving aside for the moment the novel and sophisticated aspects of his arguments, let us look at some of the more obvious reasons which can explain the immediate popularity of Smith's work. First, his words and sentences were selected with such pungency and bite as to appeal to ordinary men not accustomed to the company of academics:

> By means of glasses, hot beds, and hotwalls, very good grapes can be raised in Scotland, and very good wine too can be made of them at about thirty times the expense for which at least equally good can be brought from foreign countries. Would it be a reasonable law to prohibit the importation of all foreign wines, merely to encourage the making of Claret and Burgundy in Scotland?

Such was the direct and challenging style by which Smith broke down the barriers to communication between himself and his readers.

Of Smith's general system of economics, it is true that the individual components were not new. Obviously he had drawn upon French economists, such as Cantillon, Quesnay and Turgot. British influences upon Smith patently included those of Mandeville, Petty, Steuart and Hume. For his basic philosophy he leaned particularly upon his tutor at Glasgow University, the "never to be forgotten" Hutcheson. Smith's greatest personal achievement was to weld these individual components into one exciting whole; and one which, as we have seen, because of its down-to-earth, commonsensical approach, appealed to the ordinary reader as well as to the academic.

Not only was Smith's style direct, it was also entertaining, colorful and often amusing. He was master of the apt phrase. The publishers of *The Oxford Book of Quotations* have selected from *The Wealth of Nations* the following:

> To found a great empire for the sole purpose of raising up a people of customers, may at first sight appear a project fit only for a nation of shopkeepers. It is, however, a project altogether unfit for a nation of shopkeepers; but extremely fit for a nation whose government is influenced by shopkeepers.

It must be remembered that Smith's economics were presented in a far different way from that of the narrow technical writer and specialist which so easily frightens off the layman today. Smith's argument was graced with literary elegance that made it palatable. But the literary style served the economics; the latter was not sacrificed for the sake of the former.

> There are some very agreeable and beautiful talents of which the possession commands a certain

sort of admiration; but of which the exercise for the sake of gain is considered, whether from reason or prejudice, as a sort of public prostitution. The pecuniary recompense, therefore, of those who exercise them in this manner, must be sufficient not only to pay for the time, labour, and expense of acquiring the talents, but for the discredit which attends the employment of them as the means of subsistence. The exorbitant rewards of players, opera-singers, opera-dancers, etc., are founded upon those two principles: the rarity and beauty of the talents, and the discredit of employing them in this manner.

Smith's argument was richly illuminated with historical illustration and contemporary example. Indeed, *The Wealth of Nations* started out not as a book on economics but, according to the contemporary biographer, Dugald Stewart, as an "essay in conjectural history." By this was meant the systematic study of the effects of legal, institutional and general environmental conditions upon human progress, a branch of study which had started with Montesquieu and was taken up not only by Smith, but also by his Scottish friends and colleagues, Lords Kames, Hume, Ferguson and Millar. This field of study today would be called sociological evolutionism, and there is no doubt of Adam Smith's preoccupation with it throughout his book. His readers are continually treated to elaborate accounts of the differences in character between rural and urban population, barbarous and civilized states, the foundation of rank and precedency in rude as well as civilized societies, the peculiarities of ecclesiastical government and the effect of geography upon national character and power.

Smith lived in the days when it was still possible for an

individual to hold sway over a wide domain of knowledge. Smith himself was widely accomplished in the fields of science, art and philosophy. Besides being the author of belles-lettres on poetry, aesthetics and literary appreciation, Smith had written essays which were the foundation of a grandiose plan of a "History of the Liberal Sciences and Elegant Arts." But his fame was first firmly secured by the publication of the philosophical work, *The Theory of Moral Sentiments*, in 1759. It was in this earlier work that Smith had already made a full investigation into the ethics and philosophy, as distinct from the economics, of riches. We shall later draw considerably from this relatively neglected writing, since it provides a rich source of evidence on Smith's personality, as well as on the evolution of his thought.

When we deal with Smith's economics, we notice how its expression radiates the love of classical scholarship which he sustained throughout his life. Thus, in his chapter in *The Wealth of Nations* on the economics of wages:

> Isocrates, in what is called his discourse against the sophists, reproaches the teachers of his own times with inconsistency. "They make the most magnificent promises to their scholars, says he, and undertake to teach them to be wise, to be happy, and to be just, and in return for so important a service they stipulate the paltry reward of four or five minae. They who teach wisdom, continues he, ought certainly to be wise themselves; but if any man were to sell such a bargain for such a price, he would be convicted of the most evident folly."

Further biographical details of Adam Smith's life will help to explain further the evolution of his ideas and to give us a fuller understanding of the great eighteenth-century classic which he produced. Adam Smith was born in the small town of Kirkcaldy, on the coast of Scotland a few miles north of Edinburgh, in January, 1723. His father, who had died only a few weeks before, had been Scottish Judge Advocate and Comptroller of Customs. After an education at Kirkcaldy burgh school, Smith went to Glasgow University and matriculated there in November, 1737 at the age of fourteen. In 1740 he was elected to an Exhibition at Balliol College, Oxford. He began his teaching life in Edinburgh, where from 1748 to 1751 he delivered public lectures which were sponsored by influential friends. From 1751 to 1763 he lectured in moral philosophy at the University of Glasgow. Then, in 1764, he left Glasgow for London en route to France as tutor to the Duke of Buccleuch. With his protégé, Smith met and conversed with many eminent French writers and philosophers, including Voltaire, Turgot, Quesnay, Helvétius and Dupont. Smith returned to Scotland in 1767 and spent most of his time working on *The Wealth of Nations*, which he had begun to write in France. By this time he was receiving a substantial pension from the Duke of Buccleuch which enabled him to devote himself entirely to his writing. In 1778 he became Commissioner of Customs in Edinburgh, an appointment which he held for the remaining years of his life. He died at Edinburgh in 1790, outliving his mother by only six years.

The present chapter opened with a reference to the preparations now being made in Glasgow for the bicentenary of Adam Smith's *The Wealth of Nations*. What of the first centenary of Smith's work in 1876? It has already been explained that the triumph of free trade policies down to the middle of the nineteenth century developed with such vigor as to defy

much of Smith's own pessimism. We must now record the
strong reaction in the last half of the nineteenth century.
The extent to which the extension of the franchise in 1867,
fluctuations in economic activity and the technological development of overseas competitors played a part in this reaction is a matter for individual judgement. Whatever the reasons, Adam Smith's disciples found themselves increasingly
outnumbered after the late 1860's.

Ample testimony to this setback can be found in the
records of the centenary celebration in honor of *The Wealth
of Nations* organized by the Political Economy Club of London in 1876. The meeting addressed itself to the question:
"What are the more important results which have followed
from the publication of *The Wealth of Nations* just one hundred years ago, and in what principal directions do the
doctrines of that book still remain to be applied?" The discussion was opened by Sir Robert Lowe, Chancellor of the Exchequer in the Gladstone Government of 1868-1874, and was
presided over by Mr. Gladstone himself. After many acknowl-
edgements of the achievements of the preceding century,
several speakers referred to the prevailing reaction towards
dirigisme. Mr. Gladstone expressed the view that economists of his day had the urgent duty of "propagating opinions which shall have the effect of confining government
within its proper province. . . ." William Newmarch, the
treasurer of the club, lamented: "The full development of
the principles of Adam Smith has been in no small danger for
some time past; and one of the great dangers which now
hangs over this country is that the wholesome, spontaneous
operation of human interests and human desires seems to be
in course of rapid supersession by the erection of one government department after another, by the setting up of one set

of inspectors after another, and by the whole time of parliament being taken up in attempting to do for the nation those very things which, if the teaching of the man whose name we are celebrating today is to bear any fruit at all, the nation can do much better for itself."

But Adam Smith's reign was not, and is not, by any means over. Although by 1876 there were distinct monopolistic trends within the country, British foreign trade was to enjoy substantial freedom right up to the Import Duties Act of 1932. And even the 1930's did not set the seal upon events. Since 1945 there has been an important revival in free trade thinking. Britain's participation in the general agreement on tariffs and trade (G.A.T.T.) and in the European Free Trade Association (E.F.T.A) demonstrates her willingness to reduce tariffs by international agreement. As a result of G.A.T.T. negotiations between 1947 and 1962 the United Kingdom reduced, or bound itself not to increase, customs duties on goods which account for about one half of its ordinary imports from the other contracting countries. American participation in trade liberation has been impressive. In the Kennedy Round negotiations of 1967 forty-nine countries were involved, counting the E.E.C. as one and including India, eastern block countries and most of the South American states. Between 1968 and 1972 these countries will make tariff cuts averaging between 35 per cent and 40 per cent and extending over 75 per cent or more of the trade in industrial goods carried on between the major participating countries. The American decision to resort to taxation rather than import restrictions as a means of meeting its balance of payments problem in 1968 was a significant measure of the way in which protectionist interests are being kept at bay. Meanwhile, domestic anti-monopoly legislation in many countries, legislation which has no doubt been led by the pioneering anti-trust activity dating from 1890 in America, provides yet another powerful sign of re-acknowledgement of Adam Smith's principles.

This is not to say that new circumstances have not brought with them new problems. But it should be recognized that Adam Smith was not as doctrinaire as is sometimes believed. Prepared to consider exceptions to general rules, he was a careful *advocate*, and not, like the subsequent writers in the Manchester School, an *apostle* of free trade. Indeed, in conceding that tariffs were in some circumstances acceptable, he provides an interesting ancestry of many modern economists who have developed what they call "second best" arguments in favor of limited protectionism. Smith's general conclusion, however, was that apart from the stated exceptions there was an underlying presumption in favor of free trade and that, generally, the onus was upon interested parties to prove otherwise.

A study of Adam Smith will always be rewarding for any age. If his many brilliant contemporaries and friends such as Hume, Gibbon and Burke have earned a place in our intellectual heritage, the more so has he. For, as the biographer Francis Hirst has argued, most of them, unlike Smith, were in a certain sense men of the past. "Though their radiance can never fade, their influence wanes. But Smith has issued from the seclusion of a professorship of morals, from the drudgery of a commissionership of customs, to sit in the council chamber of princes. His word has rung through the study to the platform. It has been proclaimed by the agitator, conned by the statesman, and printed in a thousand statutes."

CHAPTER II

Kirkcaldy Upbringing

ADAM SMITH, the father of the economist, was born in 1679. By profession a solicitor, he was appointed as private secretary in Lord Loudon's Ministry; later he became Judge Advocate for Scotland. He was married in about 1707 and had a first son, Hugh, in 1709. His first wife died in 1718. By this time he was firmly settled in Kirkcaldy, having held the post of Comptroller of Customs there for four years. In Kirkcaldy he had many friends among the Fifeshire lairds. One of these was John Douglas of Strathenry, whose sister, Margaret Douglas, he married in 1720. This marriage was tragically short. Adam Smith senior died in January 1723. Only a few weeks later his bereaved young wife Margaret gave birth to a son, Adam Smith, the future author of *The Wealth of Nations*.[1]

According to the contemporary biographer, Dugald Stewart, the constitution of the infant was infirm and sickly ". . . and required all the tender solicitude of his surviving parent. She was blamed for treating him with an unlimited indulgence, but it produced no unfavourable effects on his temper or his disposition; and he enjoyed the rare satisfaction of being able to repay her affection, by every attention that filial gratitude could dictate, during the long period of sixty years."[2]

There is only scanty material available on the boyhood of Adam Smith. One anecdote (apparently authentic) relates to an event in his life when he was only three years old. His mother often used to visit her brother at Strathenry, a few miles north of Kirkcaldy. One day, left to amuse himself around the door of the house, the infant Adam Smith was stolen by a party of gypsies. The alarm was soon given and after an initial search a neighbor arrived "who had met a gypsy woman a few miles down the road carrying a child that was crying piteously." The woman, on being overtaken in a nearby wood, put down the child and fled. Prudent biographers would leave it at that; not so John Rae, who solemnly observes: "He would have made, I fear, a poor gypsy."

The town of Kirkcaldy has been traditionally called by the Scots the "lang toon," this because of its long high street that runs parallel with the seashore only a few yards away. Adam Smith was born in one of its houses and was later to write *The Wealth of Nations* in another. Out of their back windows could be seen the bustling activity of the seaport. Ships would be exporting locally mined salt and coal to the continent and bringing back scrap iron to be used especially in the nail-making manufactories. As Scottish trade grew, the demand for ships increased and Kirkcaldy's shipbuilding prospered. Likewise, the demand for Kirkcaldy nails, used in shipbuilding, increased to such an extent that at one time the town had a near monopoly of the trade.

Kirkcaldy had a flourishing town council upon which Adam Smith's uncle, Hecules Smith, sat. The town's officers included the usual Provost, Baillie and Dean of Guild. One of the council's duties was to advise the magistrates "about proper measures for employing the poor in work and preventing them from begging from door to door." It communicated its messages in the streets by beat of drum or sound of trumpet or bell: "Our brother, John Tosh, has departed and is to be buried the morn at 2 o'clock, and it's expected that you'll a' attend at the next warning of the bell."[3]

Another responsibility of the town council was the burgh school only a few paces from Adam Smith's house in the High Street. It was this school that Adam Smith attended as a boy, from the years 1729 to 1737. When the present writer visited Kirkcaldy in the summer of 1966 he found the school building in the final stages of demolition. On the one remaining wall there was a rather sad looking plaque carrying the announcement:

Here Adam Smith LLD Author of The Wealth of Nations was a pupil 1729-37.

Robert Adam, eminent architect and court architect to King George III attended this school 1734-1739.

Thomas Carlyle was school master 1816-1818.

School closed 1843.

Another pupil of the school, and one who attended at the same time as Adam Smith, was John Drysdale, the minister's son who later became Chaplain to the King and Moderator of the General Assembly. Drysdale was a lifelong friend of Smith, and it was from his brother, George Drysdale, another school fellow, that Dugald Stewart obtained brief verbal testimony of Adam Smith's schoolboy personality. Apparently, Smith soon attracted the notice of his companions in his earliest years at the school "by his passion for books, and by the extraordinary powers of his memory. The weakness of his bodily constitution prevented him from partaking in their more active amusements; but he was much beloved by them on account of his temper, which, though warm, was to an uncommon degree friendly and generous. Even then he was remarkable for those habits which remained with him through life, of speaking to himself when alone, and of *absence* in company."

If these early years do not give much in the way of biographical detail of our author, they do of his book. How dependent the writer of *The Wealth of Nations* was upon his Kirkcaldy experience and the environment of his early life is obvious at every turn. Although when taken out of the context of the general arguments of the book some details considered in isolation may look a little bizarre, nevertheless, one or two examples will help to prepare the canvas.

A seaport town, Kirkcaldy's prosperity depended on the development of commerce; it seems to have been a natural circumstance that a champion of free trade should have been raised in such an environment. Sailors, salters, colliers, nailmakers, smugglers—all these were among Smith's boyhood familiars and all of them were to appear in *The Wealth of Nations:*

Sailors: "Their wages are not greater than those of common labourers. . . . A tender mother, among the inferior ranks of people, is often afraid to send her son to school at a sea-port town, lest the sight of the ships and the conversation and adventures of the sailors should entice him to go to sea."

Colliers: "A collier working by the piece is supposed, at Newcastle, to earn commonly about double, and in many parts of Scotland about three times the wages of common labour. His high wages arise altogether from the hardship, disagreeableness and dirtiness of his work."

Nailmakers: The first three chapters of *The Wealth of Nations* contain the classic statement and analysis of the economic advantages of the division of labor. The industry of pin-making, though a "trifling" one, was selected to illustrate the economies of specialization because it had impressed him the most dramatically. It was contrasted with another small-scale industry, that of nail-making, which he said did not enjoy the same progress in these respects.

> . . . in the way in which this business [pin-making] is now carried on, not only the whole work is a peculiar trade, but it is divided into a number of branches, of which the greater part are likewise peculiar trades. One man draws out the wire, another straights it . . . a third cuts, a fourth points it, a fifth grinds it at the top for receiving the head. . . .[4]

On the other hand:

> The making of a nail . . . is by no means one of the simplest operations. The same person blows the bellows, stirs or mends the fire as there is occasion, heats the iron, and forges every part of the nail. . . . The different operations into which the making of a pin . . . is subdivided, are all of them much more simple, and the dexterity of the person, of whose life it has been the sole business to perform them, is usually much greater.

Smugglers and Customs Officers: In eighteenth-century Britain, when duties were levied on as many as twelve hundred articles, the system of customs became unwieldy and complicated. This, of course, was largely the fruit of the mid-eighteenth-century mercantile system, the great object of attack in Smith's work. The policy of the mercantile system, it will be remembered, was to boost exports and discourage imports. Accordingly, the greater part of the older duties which had been imposed on exports had gradually been reduced. Domestic traders dealing in imports could claim repayments (drawbacks) of duties when the goods were rapidly exported. An increasing number of goods for export began to enjoy bounties. The restriction on imports on the other hand was in some cases so severe as to amount to complete prohibition. Such restrictions, as Adam Smith pointed out, served only to encourage smuggling. Bounties and drawbacks gave occasion to numerous frauds; in order to obtain the bounty or drawback, goods were often shipped and sent to sea, but soon afterwards "clandestinely re-landed in some other part of the country."

It is not surprising that customs officials were a busy and important class of people. Smuggling in Scotland was encouraged by some of the lairds and the period was generally one of violence.

> Not many people are scrupulous about smuggling, when, without perjury, they can find any easy and safe opportunity of doing so. To pretend to have any scruple about buying smuggled goods, though a manifest encouragement to the violation of the revenue laws, and to the perjury which almost always attends it, would in most countries be regarded as one of those pedantic pieces of hypocrisy which, instead of gaining credit with any body, serve only to expose the person who affects to prac-

tise them, to the suspicion of being a greater knave than most of his neighbours. By this indulgence of the public, the smuggler is often encouraged to continue a trade which he is thus taught to consider as in some measure innocent; and when the severity of the revenue laws is ready to fall upon him, he is frequently disposed to defend with violence, what he has been accustomed to regard as his just property. From being at first, perhaps, rather imprudent than criminal, he at last too often becomes one of the hardiest and most determined violators of the laws of society. (II. p. 514)

Customs officials were compensated for the many risks they had to face by the granting of many perquisites. Collectors and comptrollers, for instance, were entitled to receive one shilling each to the pound of the value of uncustomed goods which they detected. In *The Wealth of Nations* Adam Smith complained that the administrative costs of collection amounted in some cases to over 30 per cent of the net revenue received by the government: ". . . the perquisites of custom house officers are everywhere much greater than their salaries; at some ports more than double or triple those salaries."

By the ruin of the smuggler, his capital, which had before been employed in maintaining productive labour, is absorbed either in the revenue of the state or in that of the revenue-officer, and is employed in maintaining unproductive, to the diminution of the general capital of the society, and of the useful industry which it might otherwise have maintained. (II. p. 515)

Such forthright words lead us on to the most striking ironies in the life of their author. For he was brought up and educated on money earned by a father, a customs man in the official duty of pursuing and arresting smugglers! And we know from the will that his father died a fairly rich man, though in his early forties. Indeed, the expenses of his funeral amounted to £80, a fact which might well have much grieved the economist son! The expenses included numerous bottles of ale, "horse hyre with wine from Kinghorn," £28 to "Deacon Lessels for the coffin and ironwork" and £25 for "money sent to Edinburgh for bisquet, stockings, and necessars."[5]

Many, if not most, of the relations on the father's side were employed in the customs service. Thus, there were Smiths who were eighteenth-century Collectors at Alloa and Montrose, and another relative by marriage was Collector at Aberdeen. The crowning irony is that the author of *The Wealth of Nations* himself, after all his labors in the interests of free trade, was rewarded by his countrymen towards the end of his life with the appointment of Commissioner of Customs for Scotland. With what kind of will and determination, one wonders, did *he* harry the smugglers!

A final illustration of Kirkcaldy boyhood environment upon the book will be taken from his school experience. But what, it may be thought, has a municipal school to do with free trade? In Book V of *The Wealth of Nations* Smith reviews what he thinks are the legitimate functions of government and what are the limitations upon his principle of natural liberty. Among governmental duties he includes that of the provision for education of the masses. Local governments, he says, should oblige parents to send their children to school and should raise taxes to provide mainly the school building. Adam Smith appealed to the experience of the Scottish legislation which by an Act in 1696 had ordained the setting up of schools in Scotland ". . . by the advice of the heritors and minister of the parish . . ." and had authorized a local rate to provide finance. "In Scotland," claimed Smith, "the establishment of such parish schools has taught almost the whole common people to read, and a very great portion of them to write and account." (II. p. 388)

But what stands out in Smith's proposals is that although he wanted to bring education within reach of all, he did not want to make it an entirely free education. Scholars were to pay fees according to their ability, ". . . the master being partly but not wholly, or even principally paid by the public; because if he was wholly, or even principally paid by it, he would soon learn to neglect his business." (II. p. 388)

To the present-day reader it is fascinating to see how the classical economists of the nineteenth century strongly reflected Smith on this point. Thus in his 1828 edition of *The Wealth of Nations*, the Scottish economist McCulloch agreed with Smith that the maintenance of a fee system would "secure the constant attendance of a person who shall be able to instruct the young, and who shall have the strongest interest to perfect himself in his business, and to attract the greatest number of scholars to his school." Similarly, the economist Thomas Malthus argued that if each child had to pay a fixed sum, "the school master would then have a stronger interest to increase the number of his pupils."

Smith believed that the average parent could detect when his child was receiving an inefficient education. The possibility of his withdrawing his child and transferring the fees to another school enabled the parent to exercise sanctions upon a potentially inefficient school. Smith himself attended school at a time when parents had been doing just this and the school was consequently being prodded into improving its ways. The school's attempts at reform were fortunately most successful during the period of Smith's attendance. Kirkcaldy had been to great lengths to secure from a neighboring town a highly reputed teacher by the name of David Miller. In 1733, under the new master, the school regulations were revised. Latin was one of the subjects taught, and the *Eutropius* which Smith used as a class book still exists and contains his autograph with the date of 1733. By the time he left in 1737 he had at least four years' training in the classics.

It is interesting that long after Smith had left the school its reputation began once more to decline.[6] In 1765 families were complaining that their children did not get their due "in the grammar school by not having been teached writing." In response, the syllabus and the fees were revised as follows:

Table of Fees per Quarter

English by itself:	one shilling and sixpence
English writing and vulgar arithmetic with one hour of writing daily:	two shillings
Latin by itself:	three shillings
Latin with writing and arithmetic:	three shillings and sixpence
Latin and Greek or Greek verse:	five shillings
Decimal arithmetic, mensuration, trigonometry and algebra:	three shillings
Church music (on occasion):	gratis

Such discriminatory pricing developed to such a degree that Robert Lowe observed (approvingly) in the following century: "In Scotland they sell education like a grocer sells figs."

Smithian philosophy on this subject was by no means confined to Scotland. It strongly influenced the development of educational policy in England before 1870. Down to about this date too, it was prominent in several states of America. It is often forgotten, for instance, that ordinary working-class parents were still paying fees for the education of their children in New York State only a century ago, and moreover only a tiny percentage of families were refusing to do so even though education was not yet compulsory. In 1849 parental fees (known as rate bills) returned over five hundred thousand dollars, which amounted to nearly one-third of the total expenditure on schools. In his annual report for 1831, the Superintendent of New York State Common Schools justified this system by an appeal to the experience of the Scottish system as described for him by one of Adam Smith's classical economics disciples: "Of the three modes of providing for popular instruction—that in which the scholars pay everything and the public nothing—that in which the public pays everything and the scholars nothing—and that in which the burden is shared by both; the exposition given by Dr. Chalmers, in the Considerations on the System of Parochial Schools in Scotland (*Edinburgh Review*, No. 91) in favour of the last, appears to us unanswerable." But Dr. Chalmers had got it from Smith; and Smith had got it from a mixture of common sense and personal experience.

CHAPTER III

Student at Glasgow and Oxford

IN 1737 Smith left the grammar school of Kirkcaldy for the University of Glasgow, where he was to remain for the next three years. The age of fourteen will seem to the modern reader extremely young for university entry; yet Adam Smith was in fact older than the average entrant in his day. Indeed, in the first half of the eighteenth century it was common for youths to enter as early as twelve. It is quite probable, especially in view of Smith being an only child and not enjoying good health, that his mother arranged for him to live in Glasgow with the family of a relative or in the house of a professor. Glasgow was then a city with a population ten times as big as Smith's native Kirkcaldy. Its tobacco trade was thriving and industry in general was beginning to enjoy a new prosperity, and by all accounts it enjoyed beautiful views, wide streets and fine buildings.

While the city was thus growing in commercial stature, Glasgow University, or "the College" as it was then called, was beginning to stage an intellectual renaissance, later to be acknowledged throughout the western world. Three professors in particular were already drawing students from all over

Europe: Alexander Dunlop, Professor of Greek; Robert Simson, Professor of Mathematics; and Francis Hutcheson, Professor of Moral Philosophy. Adam Smith studied under and was strongly influenced by all three. The most powerful influence, however, was that of Hutcheson. It is certainly from him that our economist seems to have acquired the feeling and respect for "natural liberty and justice."

Hutcheson was at this time beginning to be regarded with suspicion by the older generation of professors, in the sense that he was considered a serious danger to all their influential Puritan strongholds. Their fears were well founded. Hutcheson became, in fact, the greatest challenge to the traditional gloomy Calvinism that had ever confronted Scottish academic life. It is clear from his *System of Moral Philosophy*, published after his death, that he considered man primarily as a *social* animal; to him the science of individual ethics was inseparable from the science of politics. Like Adam Smith who followed him, Hutcheson was a reformer and a libertarian. Both strongly believed that society could be better organized and governed by the practical application of reason; and not only *could* this be done, but it *should* be done. Hutcheson it was, not Bentham, who originated the famous phrase, "the greatest happiness of the greatest number."

In Smith's first year at Glasgow, Hutcheson was persecuted by the local Presbytery for teaching his students that the standard of moral goodness was the promotion of the happiness of others. In the eyes of authority this was seen as a contravention of his subscription to the Westminster Confession. He was further reproached for contending that we could have a knowledge of good and evil without a knowledge of God. Hutcheson, however, was a hero in the eyes of the students and was defended in a formal appearance by them before the Presbytery. Many other students besides Adam Smith left his lectures imbued with the same love of liberty, reason and free speech which he himself so strongly possessed. But Hutcheson's sparkling personality apparently played an equal part. Moreover, he was the first in the University to abandon the practice of lecturing in Latin. His animated delivery in English to large audiences, and his manner of walking up and down among his class, are said to have created something of an academic revolution in eighteenth-century teaching.[1]

After three years at Glasgow, Adam Smith was awarded a prize which was intended only for the very best students at the University. This was a scholarship for Oxford. The money came from the bequest of an old Glasgow student, a devout Churchman, and it was intended for the purpose of educating Scotsmen for the service of the Church in Scotland. In Smith's time the scholarship, known as the Snell Foundation (after its founder), was worth £40 a year and was tenable for eleven years.

Smith left Scotland for Oxford in the summer of 1740, journeying on horseback the whole way, and venturing for the first time out of his native country. This year must have been a most memorable one for him. From the moment he crossed the border it is said that he was much impressed with the great superiority of English agriculture compared with that of his own country. Scottish cattle in particular were lean and poor in contrast to the fat oxen of England. We have Smith's own word that the first day he dined at the hall of Balliol College, Oxford, he was roused from one of his fits of absent-mindedness by one of the servitors who told him to "fall to, for he had never seen such a piece of beef in Scotland."

In striking contrast with Glasgow, Smith found Oxford a place of intellectual stagnation. Energy was being dissipated in petty quarrels between the colleges and in Jacobite intrigues. Scotsmen were particularly unpopular in England at this time and nowhere more so than at Balliol. Consequently, Smith led a rather secluded life and his friends consisted largely of scholars who were his compatriots. Smith's hostility to Oxford's educational inefficiency and expensiveness is well brought out in his letters of this period:

Adam Smith to William Smith "at the Duke of Argyle's House in Brutin St." Oxon: Aug. 24, 1740.

Sir,
    I yesterday receiv'd your letter with a bill of sixteen pounds enclos'd, for which I humbly thank you, but more for the good advice you were pleas'd to give me. I am indeed afraid that my expenses at college must necessarily amount to a much greater sum this year than at any time hereafter, because of the extraordinary and most extravagant fees we are obliged to pay the College and University on our admittance; it will be his own fault if any one should endanger his health at Oxford by excessive study, our only business here being to go to prayers twice a day and to lecture twice a week.

I am, dear Sir,

Your most oblig'd Servant

Adam Smith.

The incompetence of Oxford University was to be fully exposed in *The Wealth of Nations*. Adam Smith's dislike of those systems of public education wherein the teachers received a salary quite independent of their efforts was nowhere so vigorously expressed as in his verdict on the endowment (educational bequest) system, under which the universities were largely financed. Smith complained: "The endowments of schools and colleges have diminished more or less the necessity of application in the teachers. Their subsistence, so far as it arises from their salaries, is evidently derived from a fund altogether independent of their success and reputation in their particular professions." (II. p. 365)

Compared with their Scottish counterparts, English universities relied much more upon endowments than upon fees for their finance. Fee paying allowed much choice between teachers of varying efficiency. Under these circumstances Smith argued that it would be unpleasant for a teacher to observe the greater part of his students deserting his lectures and those that stayed treating him with obvious contempt and derision. The endowment system curtailed this choice and it allowed the teachers to protect themselves against the above discomforts.

> A teacher, instead of explaining to his pupils himself the science in which he proposes to instruct them may read some book upon it; and if this book is written in a foreign and dead language, by interpreting it to them into their own; or, what would give him still less trouble, by making them interpret it to him, and by now and then making an occasional remark upon it, he may flatter himself that he is giving a lecture. The slightest degree of knowledge and application will enable him to do this, without exposing himself to contempt or derision, or saying anything that is really foolish, absurd or ridiculous. The discipline of the college, at

the same time, may enable him to force all his
pupils to the most regular attendance upon this
sham-lecture, and to maintain the most decent and
respectful behaviour during the whole time of the
performance. (II. p. 369)

In such words did Smith return his treatment as a youth at
Oxford; for there is no doubt at all that Oxford University
was the prominent example in his mind in this part of *The
Wealth:* "In the University of Oxford, the greater part of the
public professors have, for these many years, given up altogether even the pretence of teaching." (II. p. 367)

Obviously, there was no Hutcheson *there,* and the contrast
so far from home must have been pitiful. The attack in *The
Wealth* is piled on with increasing bitterness. Smith insisted
that the process of graduating at a university consisted merely
of doing time. "The privileges of graduates are a sort of statutes of apprenticeship. . . ." (II. p. 368). The discipline of
colleges and universities was generally contrived, not for the
benefit of the students, but for the interest, ". . . or more
properly speaking, for the ease of the masters." It was not
surprising that improvements in the different branches of
philosophy were being made outside the endowed Universities. Even when the improvements were made the Universities were not very forward in adopting them. Such was their
comfortable slumber, Smith asserted, that they had become
". . . sanctuaries in which exploded systems and obsolete
prejudices found shelter and protection, after they had been
hunted out of every corner of the world." (II. p. 377)

The inefficiency of the teaching at Oxford drove Smith back
upon his own resources. He read deeply and widely in several
subjects and in many languages. It was fortunate that Balliol
at least possessed one of the best college libraries at Oxford.

Smith turned away from the mathematics in which he had developed an interest at Glasgow, partly no doubt because he could get no one to continue teaching it to him. He devoted most of his energies to the ancient Latin and Greek classics, in which the Balliol library was particularly well stocked. In later life he was to surprise many people by his great depth of knowledge of this literature. He told Dugald Stewart that while at Oxford he employed himself frequently in the practice of translation (particularly from the French) with a view to the improvement of his own style. His knowledge of foreign languages was obtained, not in order that he could make a "vain parade of tasteless erudition," but to gain acquaintance with everything "that could illustrate the institutions, the manners, and the ideas of different ages and nations."

But even such private time was occasionally invaded. It is said that one day Smith was detected reading Hume's *Treatise of Human Nature* and was punished by a severe reprimand and the confiscation of what was then considered to be an evil book. These were the days, it must be remembered, when to be seen entertaining the notions of Deism was regarded as a crime by the University. It is not surprising that Adam Smith's enthusiasm suffered many setbacks in such an unfriendly environment. On November 29, 1743, he wrote to his mother, "I am just recovered from a violent fit of lazyness, which has confined me to my elbow-chair these three months." In July, 1744, he wrote telling her that he had been suffering from scurvy and shaking in the head but that "it had now been cured by taking tar-water."

Adam Smith left Oxford, never to return, in 1746. There are several possible reasons why he left before the expiration of his scholarship. One is that the discontent with his surroundings became more acute; some of the consequences of the Scottish Rebellion may have aggravated his position in a Jacobite college. (Adam Smith always expressed strong opinions in favor of the Revolution settlement.) Another reason which might explain his early departure from Oxford is that it is very possible that he had decided by this time, the influences of Hutcheson and Hume having now worked deeply upon him, that he could not now fulfil the conditions of his scholarship and go on with his studies for the Church. In the words of Dugald Stewart, "he chose to consult in this instance his own inclination, in preference to the wishes of his friends; and abandoning at once all the schemes which their prudence had formed for him, he resolved to return to his own country, and to limit his ambition to the uncertain prospect of obtaining, in time, some one of those moderate preferments to which literary attainments lead in Scotland."

CHAPTER IV

Professional Threshold in Edinburgh

IN the two years after he left Oxford, Adam Smith lived once more in Kirkcaldy. Now in his early twenties, he spent much of this time seeking employment. It seems that he had in mind the position of private tutor to some noble scion, a position which, in those aristocratic days, was highly remunerated. But Smith's ambition was not fulfilled. According to one biographer his failure was due to "his absent manner and bad address" and to the fact that "he seemed to the ordinary parental mind a most unsuitable person to be entrusted with the care of spirited and perhaps thoughtless young gentlemen."

Much of these two years was spent in writing. It is probable that in this period he wrote some of the belles-lettres and the essays on astronomy, ancient physics, logic and metaphysics. His *History of Astronomy* was almost certainly written at this time.[1] In it Smith began with Thales and Pythagoras and went through the systems of Copernicus, Gallileo, Kepler and Descartes to that of Sir Isaac Newton. The last-named was given a special place of honor. Newton, claimed the young Smith, was the only natural philosopher whose system contained in itself "the real chains which nature makes use of to bind together her several operations."

In 1748, at the age of 25, Smith did at last obtain employment. His good fortune was due to the influence of his friend, James Oswald, Kirkcaldy's representative in Parliament and Commissioner of the Navy. Through him Smith was introduced to Lord Kames, a leader of the Edinburgh Bar. Kames was an enthusiast not only in law but also in moral philosophy, history, literary criticism and even agriculture. Being himself self-educated, he was well conscious of the obstacles in the way of cultural and intellectual progress in his society. At a time when the desire for self-improvement and the demand for public lectures were rapidly growing in Edinburgh, he was, it seems, with the support of lawyer friends acting as a kind of intellectual impressario in the service of public education. In Adam Smith he found somebody who had not only acquired the English accent, which at this time had become fashionable in Scotland, but also a person who was well read in the prose and poetry of England. Smith, the young Oxford graduate, was accordingly appointed by Kames and his friends to give a public lecture course on English literature. The lectures were scheduled to be given in Edinburgh (only seven miles from Kirkcaldy) and were booked for the winter of 1748.

The appointment appears to have been a great success. Smith benefited not only professionally, but financially. It has been estimated that the lectures were attended by about 100 persons, each of whom paid a one guinea fee. This profitable result must have been particularly satisfying to Smith, who, in education as in so many things, was an innovator and advocate of free enterprise. Whether his sponsors covered all their costs is not clear. There is only scanty evidence, for instance, about which building was used. There is no sign from the official minutes of this period that Smith or any society had been granted a room in the University for the purpose. At this time, however, there were many private lecture rooms belonging to the numerous Edinburgh Clubs and it is probable that Smith had one of these provided for him. The most likely institution was the Philosophical Society of Edinburgh. This had been instituted in 1731 for the improvement of medical knowledge and in 1737 had extended its scope to include science and literature.[2]

The content of these literary lectures of Smith is not fully known,[3] since his own manuscripts of them were burned shortly before his death. It is recorded by James Woodrow, however, that Smith utilized parts of the Edinburgh lectures a few years later in a course delivered at Glasgow University. Woodrow, who attended this latter course, wrote to the Earl of Buchan:

> Adam Smith delivered a set of admirable lectures on language (not as a grammarian but as a rhetorician) on the different kinds of characteristics of style suited to different subjects, simple, nervous, etc., the structure, the natural order, the proper arrangement of the different members of the sentence etc. He characterised the style and the genius of some of the best of the ancient writers and poets, but especially historians, Thucydides, Polybius, etc. translating long passages of them, also the style of the best English classics, Lord Clarendon, Addison, Swift, Pope, etc. . . . his remarks and rules given in the lectures I speak of, were the result of a fine taste and sound judgement, well calculated to

be exceedingly useful to young composers, so that I have often regretted that some part of them has never been published.[4]

From incidental remarks of Smith's friends we can get a little more idea of his literary opinions at this time. He was obviously in the conservative tradition of Dryden, Pope and Gray and his opinions were not a matter of indifference to other poets and critics. Wordsworth, in the preface to his *Lyrical Ballads,* speaking for the new romantic poets, calls Smith "the worst critic, David Hume excepted, that Scotland, a soil to which this sort of weed seems natural, has produced." Boswell, who also attended the literary lectures by Smith in Glasgow, told Samuel Johnson of Smith's dislike of blank verse. "They do well to call it blank," Smith had said, "for blank it is. I myself even, who never could find a single rhyme in my life, could make blank verse as fast as I could speak." Johnson was delighted with this report and exclaimed, "Sir, I was once in company with Smith, and we did not take to each other; had I known that he loved rhyme as much as you tell me he does, I should have hugged him."

Smith at this time was also laying the foundations of his writing career. The Foulis Press of Edinburgh had commissioned him to collect and edit the works of the Scottish poet, Hamilton. Hamilton was an exiled Jacobite who had been poet laureate to the Young Pretender in 1745. Smith acted as an anonymous editor and, though no Jacobite himself, he did not let politics stand in the way of artistic appreciation. "It is hoped," Smith wrote in the preface, "that the many beauties of language and sentiment, which appear in this little volume, and the fine genius the author everywhere discovers, will make it acceptable to every reader of taste, and will in

some measure atone for our presumption in presenting the
public with poems, of which none have the author's finishing
hand, and many of them only first essays in his early youth."
The poet was pardoned in 1750, two years after publication,
and on returning to Scotland struck up a happy friendship
with Smith. Ill health, however, soon sent him abroad again,
to the south of France, where he died of consumption in
1754.

The sponsors of Adam Smith's public lectures in Edinburgh belonged to a growing class of gentry-intellectuals who
had a strong interest in the promotion not only of the cultural but also of the economic life of Scotland at this time.
Besides Lord Kames and James Oswald, there were Sir William Pulteney, Robert Craigie and Alexander Wedderburn,
who later became Chancellor of the Exchequer. Like Smith,
they can be described as individualist thinkers in the Stoic
tradition; many of them, being lawyers, had a strong desire to
develop the cultural and philosophical aspects of the legal
profession. Adam Smith explains their need in his first book,
The Theory of Moral Sentiments: ". . . it might have been
expected that the reasonings of lawyers upon the different imperfections and improvements of the laws of different countries should have given occasion to an enquiry into what were
the natural rules of justice, independent of all positive institution. It might have been expected that these reasonings
should have led them to aim at establishing a system of what
might properly be called natural jurisprudence, or a theory
of the general principles which ought to run through, and be
the foundation of, the laws of all nations. . . ."

Accordingly, in addition to his lectures in literature, Smith
was commissioned by the same group of sponsors to give a
course on the philosophy of law. In this course he probably

surveyed the whole evolution of law in Western Europe, beginning with the Roman Empire and going through the development of feudalism, the effects of the crusades upon the distribution of property and trade, the rise of towns and the increase of liberty. Smith's survey concluded, it is believed, with an examination of the subsequent re-emergence of Roman Law and the development of commerce. At this time (1748) the Frenchman Quesnay published his *Essai Physique sur l'Economie Animale,* in which he applied the notions of natural liberty, natural order and natural rights. Simultaneously occupied with the same idea of natural liberty, Adam Smith was applying it much more to economics, and in a way which combined some of the ideas of Hutcheson with Smith's own immediate observations and awareness of the world.

A copy of some of this part of Smith's Edinburgh lecture course, written by an amanuensis, was discovered in the 1930's. It shows, for instance, that Smith was already working upon and developing his analysis of the institution of the division of labor. The following is an extract:

> When the market is very small it is altogether impossible that there can be that separation of one employment from another which naturally takes place when it is more extensive. In a country village, for example, it is altogether impossible that there should be such a trade as that of a porter. All the burdens, which, in such a situation, there can be any occasion to carry from one house to another, would not give full employment to a man for a week in the year.[5]

In contrast, Smith continues, porters in big towns had *plenty* of scope. The lecturer was drawing upon the immediate environment of his audience. According to a description of Edinburgh written in 1791, a certain number of porters stood "all day long, and most of the night, at the top of the High-Street, waiting for employment. Whoever has occasion for them, has only to pronounce the word 'Cadie,' and they fly from all parts to attend the summons."[6]

By the late 1740's, therefore, Smith's economic system was obviously under construction. In 1755 he presented a paper to a society in Edinburgh in which, according to Dugald Stewart, many of the most important opinions of *The Wealth of Nations* were detailed. The following is an extract:

> Man is generally considered by statesmen and projectors as the materials of a sort of political mechanics. Projectors disturbed nature in the course of her operations in human affairs; and it requires no more than to let her alone and give her fair play in the pursuit of her ends that she may establish her own designs. . . . Little else is requisite to carry a state to the highest degree of opulence from the lowest barbarism, but peace, easy taxes and a tolerable administration of justice; all the rest being brought about by the natural course of things. All governments which thwart this natural course, which force things into another channel, or which endeavour to arrest the progress of society at a particular point are unnatural and to support themselves are obliged to be oppressive and tyranical.

Smith's thoughts developed by the prompting of immediate teaching obligations. He tackled with particular zeal and enjoyment most of the pedagogic problems. He taught himself to be especially successful in verbal style and in the ability to command attention. It is interesting to compare his great enthusiasm in *The Wealth of Nations* about the success of the ancient Greek teachers of philosophy and rhetoric. The demand for such teaching, he says, was for a long time so small that the teachers could not find constant employment in any one city but were advised to travel about from place to place. Inevitably the free market triumphed:

> The demand for such instruction produced, what it always produces, the talent for giving it; and the emulation which an unrestrained competition never fails to excite, appears to have brought that talent to a very high degree of perfection. In the attention which the ancient philosophers excited, in the empire which they acquired over the opinions and principles of their auditors, in the faculty which they possessed of giving a certain tone and character to the conduct and the conversation of those auditors; they appeared to have been much superior to any modern teachers. (II. p. 383)

In modern times, Smith continues (no doubt with Oxford again in his mind), the diligence of public teachers is more or less corrupted by the circumstances, which render them more or less independent of their success and reputation in their particular professions.

In ancient Greek society, Smith informs us, the state played only a small part. At most it gave some of the teachers a particular place to teach in; thus the Academy to Plato, the Lyceum to Aristotle and the Portico to Zeno. Even so, Smith insists, private donors also provided places in which to teach; Epicurus, for instance, bequeathed his gardens to his own school. Not until the time of Marcus Antonius, Smith records, did teachers have any salary from the public; they had what arose from the honoraries or fees of their scholars. Moreover, there was no protection in the form of licensing and there were no privileges of graduation; that is to say, there was no condition, as there was in Smith's day, that before taking up a particular trade or profession the practitioners had to show that they had attended any of the schools or classes recognized for the purpose.

> If the opinion of their own utility could not draw scholars to them the law neither forced anybody to go to them nor rewarded anybody for having gone to them. The teachers had no jurisdiction over their pupils, nor any other authority besides that natural authority, which superior virtue and abilities never fail to procure from young people towards those who are entrusted with any part of their education. (II. p. 382)

As a very young man Smith seems to have firmly decided to tread in the paths of such classical predecessors; for was not his idol, Hutcheson, in this very tradition? Smith was aware that the demand for good teaching in this period could lead to a good living, and monetary reward was not inconsistent with the noble pursuit of learning. Socrates, he is pleased to inform us, demanded about £33 from each of his scholars for one course. Similarly, Plutarch and many other eminent teachers in those times had acquired great fortunes. The teacher Gorgias, Smith observes (and with how much Scottish wistfulness?), made a present to the Temple of Delphi of his own statue in solid gold!

Plato himself is said to have lived with a good deal

of magnificence. Aristotle, after having been tutor to Alexander, and most munificently rewarded, as it is universally agreed, both by him and his father Philip, thought it worthwhile notwithstanding, to return to Athens, in order to resume the teaching of his schools. (I. p. 151)

Smith's Edinburgh lectures continued from 1748 to 1751. These three years were obviously a formative period not only in his intellectual life but also in his personal circumstances. It was at Edinburgh that he acquired a taste for club life. Long after he moved to Glasgow he made frequent journeys to Edinburgh clubs to attend meetings and to see his friends. One wonders, incidentally, what kind of a clubman he was. And why was it that he troubled to attend so many social clubs when, by all accounts, he spent so much time absent-mindedly lost in his own thoughts? Scott ventures one explanation:

> . . . at some stage in the conversation a remark caught his interest and he followed the thought on and on and became completely lost in the pursuit. Later, when he had acquired some celebrity, it became usual to attract his attention and to draw him into the discussion by a direct question or by provocative statements. On such occasions he frequently explained his view in detail, which accounts for the reports that his conversation resembled a lecture. It is not improbable that on an average of a number of meetings, he spoke less than the majority of his fellow members.[7]

CHAPTER V

Professor at Glasgow: The Literary Stylist

IN 1750 the death occurred of Mr. Loudon, Professor of Logic in Glasgow College; Adam Smith was elected to the vacancy in January, 1751. Smith's obligations at Edinburgh, however, did not allow him to start his new appointment until October. By that time the Professor of Moral Philosophy (Professor Craigie) became ill and Smith was asked to substitute for him in addition to fulfilling his new duties in the Chair of Logic. In the emergency he leaned heavily on the material that he had been using in his Edinburgh lectures. Having no great enthusiasm for the formal syllabus in Logic, Smith departed from it whenever he could. This dislike of Logic and "the abstruse syllogisms of a quibbling dialectic" had been shared by his mentor, Hutcheson. John Millar, who attended Smith's classes in Logic in 1751-52, tells us that Smith "saw the necessity of departing widely from the plan that had been followed by his predecessors, and of directing the attention of his pupils to studies of a more interesting and useful nature than the logic and the metaphysics of the schools." After explaining so much of the ancient logic as was requisite to the course, Smith "dedicated all the rest of his time to the delivery of a system of rhetoric and belles-lettres."

Long after Smith had vacated the Chair of Logic for that of Moral Philosophy he took every opportunity to continue the Rhetoric Lectures and could not resist the temptation, even in his course on Jurisprudence, to make long digressions on literary criticism. New and important evidence on Smith's lectures on Rhetoric and Belles-Lettres came to light with the discovery in 1958 of notes written by a student of Smith in the year 1762-63. These notes were edited and published by J. M. Lothian in 1963. Reading them today we get the impression of an earnest young (Smith was in his thirties) lecturer; enthusiastic, intellectual, didactic and, on first reading, particularly class-conscious. A brief survey of these lectures will help us to form a picture of the emerging personality and scholarship of the man.

It is clear that Smith had been given the task of providing an education for the sons of aristocrats and for those aspiring towards a life of gentlemanly cultivation and self-improvement. In the first lecture reported by the student (Friday, November 19, 1762), Smith demonstrates how certain gestures or "peculiarities of dress" indicate "something mean and low in those in whom we find them." He then goes on to argue that the more sophisticated can also detect class differences by the various shades of speech and vocabulary. "Perhaps nine-tenths of the people of England," argued Smith, "say 'I'se do't' instead of 'I will do it' . . . but no gentleman would use that expression without the imputation of vulgarity. We may indeed naturally expect that the better sort will often exceed the vulgar in the propriety of their language, but where there is no such excellence we are apt to prefer those in use amongst them, by the association we form betwixt their words and the behaviour we admire in them."

Smith, however, was not being obsequious to his upper-class audience or merely giving his (fee-paying) customers what they wanted to hear. He was making a serious attempt to trace the sources of language structure. In firmly established aristocracies such as Britain "the rules of purity of style" were to be drawn from the Court, to which those of the higher rank generally gravitated. Whether this was desirable or not was neither here nor there; it was a reality. In countries which, on the contrary, were divided into a number of sovereignties, a general standard of language could not be expected since the "better sort" were scattered in different places. Accordingly, in Greece and Italy each State adhered to its own dialect without yielding the preference to any other. Despite the more standardized language of Britain, however, there was still enough choice to allow an individual speaker or writer to express his particular personality. The wise man, for instance, would not in conversation affect a character that was unnatural to him. Agreeable style in authors consisted of thoughts which were justly and properly expressed "in such a manner as shows the passion they affected the author with, and so that all seemed natural and easy."[1] Swift and Addison were to be praised on this account. Lord Shaftesbury, on the other hand, failed because he had formed to himself an idea of beauty of style which was not natural to his character.

As the lectures proceed, they show Smith's strong analytic mind gradually developing a set of well-reasoned first principles. His boundless knowledge of the world of scholarship must have astonished his listeners. He shows familiarity with the great historians of both antiquity and modern times. He confidently pronounces that a certain device occurs not once, "no, not once, in the whole of Demosthenes" and that Aristotle sticks to a particular style "in his whole works."

Apart from influencing his young audience in the ways of genteel behavior and refined taste, our Glasgow professor was also given the more practical task of teaching them how to write. This particular duty was obviously giving Smith himself a useful apprenticeship in the author's craft. In the lectures we can see him developing from the mere stylist into an intellect with a burning desire to reshape, polish and sharpen the language into a serviceable tool of analytic thought. The litterateur is evolving into a social scientist. Smith continually tells his students that their expressions should be free from all ambiguity and that the words they select should be native to their own language. Consider, he says, the word "unfold." This good old English term derived from an English root was nicely expressive and easily understood. "This word, however, has within these ten years been most unaccountably thrust out of common use by a French word of not half the strength or significance, to wit, 'develop.' Though of the same signification with 'unfold' it could never convey the idea so strongly to an English reader."[2]

For a direct native style, the writing of Swift was to be commended more than any others; his language was more English than any other writer. Perspicuity demanded moreover a natural order of expression, free of parenthesis and superfluous words. Short sentences were generally more perspicuous than long ones. There were exceptions to this rule, however, especially where there was a danger of producing an unconnected way of writing. (Smith himself, throughout his work, is fond of the semicolon.) The expressive use of such ornaments of language as allegories, similes and metaphors, was apt to make an author's style "dark and perplexed." Metaphors should be used very sparingly, and even then they should be well chosen. Lord Shaftesbury typifies the author who depends too much on metaphors, which, according to Smith, lead his readers "into a dungeon of metaphorical obscurity." A *dungeon* indeed!

After about a dozen lectures, Smith is stressing with added firmness that the primary need for improvement in the use of language is precision. The perfection of style "consists in expressing, in a most concise, proper and precise manner, the thought of the author, and that in the manner which best conveys the sentiment, passion or affection with which it affects,—or he pretends it does affect—him, and which he designs to communicate to his reader. This, you'll say, is no more than common sense: and indeed it is no more."[3]

The examples from writers who deal in the passions and emotions now give way to those who are concerned to analyze events and to draw out the causes of things. From the prose writers he turns to the historians. Here Smith's erudition is displayed even more impressively. He examines, among others, Herodotus, Thucydides, Xenophon, Livy, Tacitus, Machiavelli and Clarendon. The design of historical writing, Smith tells his audience, is not merely to entertain but also to instruct. "It sets before us more interesting and important events of human life, points out the causes by which these events were brought about, and by this means points out to us by what manner and method we may produce similar good effects or avoid similar bad ones."[4] Smith promptly seizes upon the key questions: How far should the historian go in seeking the causes? Should he dwell simply on the proximate causes or should he also trace the more remote ones? Smith

illustrates with the problem of a biographer of Oliver Crom-
well, who found the events in his period "so connected with
those before the Reformation, and those again with the
former reigns, that he was obliged to go as far back as the
Conquest; and by going on in the same way he would have
found himself reduced to the necessity of tracing the whole
back even to the fall of Adam."[5] Whatever the answer to this
question, it was clear that the writer should dwell upon and
speculate upon the *causes* of events. Smith's subsequent masterpiece, it will be remembered, bore the full title of: *An
Enquiry into the Nature and Causes of The Wealth of Nations.*

The causes of events may be either external or internal,
i.e., in the minds of the chief actors. Men of action who had
been involved in the events they record, men such as Caesar,
Polybius and Thucydides, all described the external aspects.
They concerned themselves with such things as the tactical
development of a battle, the nature of the ground, the
weather, etc. Other historians, who were not men of action,
accounted for the events of battles by the circumstances that
influenced the minds of the combatants. Smith gives as an
example of the "man of action" type of history, Thucydides'
account of the attack on Syracuse by the Athenians. The second kind of historical writing is illustrated by the account
written by Tacitus of the battle between Vespasian and the
Vitellians' general.

Thucydides is obviously Adam Smith's favorite. The objec-
tive of previous historians "seems to have been rather to
amuse than to instruct." A revolution in writing occurred
with Thucydides' history of the Peloponnesian War. Smith is
impressed with the latter's claim to record in the truest manner "the various incidents of that war, and the causes that

produced it, so that posterity may learn how to produce the like events or shun others, and know what is to be expected from such and such circumstances." Thucydides excludes all irrelevancies: "The events are all chosen so as to be of consequence to the narrations, and in his account of them he abundantly satisfies his design accounting for every event by the external causes that produced it, pointing out what circumstances of time, place, etc. on the side of either party determined the success of the enterprise they were engaged in." Thucydides, moreover, is praised for being the first who pays any attention at all to civil history, in contrast to his predecessors, who concentrated merely on military history. Among the more modern historians, it was Machiavelli who, in Smith's opinion, was the only writer who had "contented himself with that which is the chief purpose of history, to relate events and connect them with their causes, without becoming a party on either side."

In the grand sweep of the Rhetoric lectures, Smith throws out provoking observations from history, sociology, politics, economics and even aesthetics. Sometimes his pronouncements involve nearly all of these at once. Consider finally his observations on dancing and poetry. These, he contended, were pastimes of the most barbarous and rude nations; they were the pursuit of primitive people who sought merriment and recreation at the end of the day. Dancing required music and as this developed so too did poetry. Poetry was a necessary attendant, "especially on vocal music."

> Thus it is that poetry is cultivated in the most rude and barbarous nations, often to considerable perfection; whereas they make no attempt towards the improvement of prose. It is the introduction of commerce, or at least of the opulence that is com-

monly the attendant of commerce, that first brings on the improvement of prose. Opulence and commerce commonly precede the improvement of arts and refinement of every sort. I do not mean that the improvement of arts and refinements of manners are the necessary consequences of commerce . . . but only that it is a necessary requisite. Wherever the inhabitants of a city are rich and opulent, where they enjoy the necessaries and conveniences of life in ease and security, there the arts will be cultivated, and refinement of manners a never-failing attendant. . . . Prose is naturally the language of business, as poetry is of pleasure and amusement. Prose is the style in which all the common affairs of life, all business and agreements, are made. No-one ever made a bargain in verse: pleasure is not what he there aims at.

CHAPTER VI

Glasgow Lectures on Republicanism, Slavery, Marriage and Justice

ALTHOUGH the subject of literary taste and style was close to Smith's heart, it was not his predominant teaching responsibility in this period. From 1752 to 1764 his main task at Glasgow was to give a course of lectures on Moral Philosophy. According to Smith's old pupil and friend John Millar, the course fell into four parts: Natural Theology, Ethics, Justice and what can be called Political Expediency. The second of these divisions (Ethics) was elaborated in Smith's book, *The Theory of Moral Sentiments* (published in 1759), which we shall examine later. Details of the last two divisions came to light with the publication in 1896 of the contents of another notebook, this time of a student who attended Smith's main lectures in 1762. These notes contain a first draft of a projected work by Smith on Justice or Jurisprudence, "a sort of theory and history of law and government," together with what amounted to germinal ideas for *The Wealth of Nations.*

In the history of economic thought the main significance of these published lectures lies in the evidence that they gave of the true originality of Smith's thought. *The Wealth of Nations* was published in 1776, and had been immediately preceded by works of French authors such as Quesnai and Turgot which contained similar economic analysis. This fact, together with the knowledge that Smith visited France in 1764, led many nineteenth-century scholars to attribute much of Smith's work to his dependence on the French authors. The publication of the Glasgow lectures of 1762, however, showed that the embryo of *The Wealth of Nations* was there in Smith's mind well before his French tour and before he had access to much of the French literature. We shall examine the lectures briefly, partly on account of their intrinsic interest and partly because of their indirect value in helping us present a comprehensive, unfolding, if indirect, biographical picture.

Smith entitled his Glasgow course of lectures *Jurisprudence*. He divided the course into four sections: Justice, Polity (Policy), Revenue and Arms.

The end of Justice, Smith argued, was to secure from injury. Men are induced to enter civil society by the two principles, authority and utility (obedience and the instinct of self-preservation). In his examination of the more abstract theories of the political philosophers—notably those of Locke and Hobbes, who believed in some form of social contract—Smith responded with characteristic scepticism and common sense. There were no grounds, he asserted, for our believing in any original contract. If ordinary people had never heard of it why should it be accepted, even notionally?

Ask a common porter or day-labourer why he

obeys the civil magistrate, he will tell you that it is right to do so, that he sees others do it, that he would be punished if he refused to do it, or perhaps it is a sin against God not to do it. But you never hear him mention a contract as the foundation of his obedience.[1]

It was of no use either to argue that ordinary people, by their habit of remaining in the country, *tacitly* consented to a contract. How could the average person avoid staying in it?

You were not consulted whether you should be born in it or not. And how can you get out of it? Most people know no other language nor country, are poor, and obliged to stay not far from the place where they were born, to labour for a subsistence. They cannot therefore be said to have given a consent to a contract, though they may have the strongest sense of obedience. (*Lectures*, p. 12)

Adam Smith traced the origins of governments through various stages; first the nation of savages, second the nation of shepherds, third the system of small clans with chieftains. Next he examined the circumstances in which aristocracies arose. After putting forward the reasons for the fall of the "little republics" he concluded with an account of the different forms of government that arose in Europe after the dissolution of "arbitrary government." The origin of republicanism particularly interested him. Before the development of a free enterprise market economy, Smith argued, ordinary people were dependent on a chieftain to whom they owed personal service. With the development of manufactures, individuals began to work not for one person but for an impersonal market. Since governments required money to continue their services, they were forced to court the interests and votes of the widely and increasingly dispersed number of "independent plebians." As the latter increased their incomes they were eventually able to bargain for and to obtain the franchise. The seeds of representative government were thus sown by the free market economy.

Smith discerned a weakness in many of the early republics, especially the smaller ones. "When in consequence of the improvement of arts, a state has become opulent, it must be reckoned a great hardship to go out to war, whereas among our ancestors it was thought no inconvenience to take the field." (*Lectures*, p. 27) Since the rich would not take the field "but on the most urgent account" it therefore became necessary to employ mercenaries and "the dregs of the people" to serve in war. "Such persons could never be trusted in war unless reduced to the form of a standing army, and subjected to rigid discipline, because their private interest was but little concerned, and therefore without such treatment they could not be expected to be very resolute in their undertakings. Gentlemen may carry on a war without much discipline, but this a mob can never do." (*Lectures*, p. 28) Such was the main explanation, thought Smith, for the downfall of Greece.

Smith's republicanism, however, was not *doctrinaire;* his general attitude was pragmatical. There was much of his friend Burke in his desire for sensible trial and error. A combination of *some* non-republican elements of government was often no bad thing. He wanted "a happy mixture of all the different forms of government properly restrained, and a perfect security to liberty and property." The pattern of government as it had evolved in eighteenth-century Britain was relatively speaking quite reasonably successful, although there was of course much room for improvement. The evolution of some separation of powers in British government was certainly a happy development. All monetary affairs had to take place in the Commons, the judges were independent of the king, while the Habeus Corpus Act provided further securities of liberty. The jury system was also a "friend of liberty."

Typical of Smith's practical and moderate approach was his desire not to be too specific on the question of the people's right of resistance to a government. He thought that Locke's stipulation that when a sovereign raises taxes against the will of the people resistance is lawful, needed cautious qualification. What *was* the will of the people after all? There were few countries where people had any vote in the matter. Even in Britain there was only a "figurative consent"; the number of voters was only a small proportion of the number of people.

> Exorbitant taxes no doubt justify resistance, for no people will allow the half of their property to be taken from them; but though the highest propriety be not observed, if they have any degree of moderation, people will not complain. (*Lectures*, p. 69)

In a section on domestic law Adam Smith considers the position of the family and the relationship between husband and wife, parent and child, master and servant. Whatever the "religious" arguments for marriage as a sanctified institution, marriage would emerge quite naturally on ordinary grounds of utility. In pre-Christian Rome, the husband had unlimited power of divorce and was not accountable for his conduct. But though he had this power it was thought contrary to good manners to exercise it. "We may observe an utility in this constitution of our nature that children have so long a dependence upon their parents, to bring down their passions to theirs, and thus be trained up at length to become useful members of society. Every child gets his piece of education, even under the most worthless parent." (*Lectures*, p. 74) The relationship between father and son in a monogomous marriage was instinctive and natural.

> The idea we have of a father does not arise from the voluptuous act which gave occasion to our existence, for this idea is partly loathsome, partly ridiculous. The real idea that a son has of a father is the director of his infancy, the supporter of his helplessness, his guardian, pattern and protector. These are the proper filial sentiments. The father's idea of a son is of one that depends upon him, and was bred up in his house or at his expense, by which connection there should grow up an affection towards him; but a spurious offspring is disagreeable from the resentment that arises against the mother's infidelity. (*Lectures*, p. 75)

Our author next considers the subject of love. This changed with the changing circumstances of society. With the passage of time ". . . love, which was formerly a ridiculous passion, became more grave and respectable." Smith offers as proof of this the observation that no ancient tragedy turned on love "whereas now it is more respectable and influences all the public entertainments. This can be accounted for only by the changes of mankind." (*Lectures*, p. 80) Where there was polygamy there was both a "jealousy of interest" and consequently "a want of tranquility." (*Lectures*, p. 81) Polygamy was "exceedingly hurtful to the populousness of a nation."

Where there are many children they cannot all have the affection of the parent "and it is only by this means that any of them can establish themselves. . . . I may regard four or five children who are connected with my friend, but if there are a hundred in the same relation they are little regarded." (*Lectures*, p. 84) "The effect of marriage is to legitimate the children." (*Lectures*, p. 89)

On the subject of slavery Adam Smith expresses himself with even more conviction than in *The Wealth of Nations*. First he reminds his students of the wide extent of slavery in their own lifetime. "We are apt to imagine that slavery is quite extirpated, because we know nothing of it in this part of the world; but even at present it is almost universal." Exploitation was always associated with a non-market situation; the operation of a market always assumes the participation of free individuals. "A free man keeps as his own whatever is above his rent, and therefore has a motive to industry. Our colonies would be much better cultivated by free men." (*Lectures*, p. 99) Even in Britain there was some element of slavery remaining. Smith illustrated with the example of bondsmen: the colliers and salters, many of whom he would have seen in his own native area of Kirkcaldy. Although they had privileges which slaves as such did not enjoy, nevertheless they were not strictly at liberty to change trades.

> The common wages of a day-labourer is between six and eight pence, that of a collier is half a crown. If they were free their prices would fall. At Newcastle the wages exceed not ten pence or a shilling, yet colliers often leave our coal-works, where they have a half a crown a day, and run there though they have less wages, where they have liberty. (*Lectures*, p. 100)

Smith analyzed the reasons why slavery was beginning to disappear in some places, especially in Western Europe. One of the reasons was the influence of the clergy, who were generally more in favor with the common people than the nobility. Sometimes a strong and enlightened monarchy would be influential. The emergence of the free market, however, was the surest cause of emancipation. Landlords at first began to lease their land to the "slaves." At harvest the crop was equally divided between landlord and tenant. The workers on the land having now more incentive to become efficient, the annual crop began to increase significantly. The landlord as well as the "slaves" clearly benefited from the deal. As this process continued the latter eventually became emancipated villeins.

In the last section of the Lectures on Justice, Adam Smith surveyed the system of private law, beginning with a summary of the Roman Law of property and the particular usages of Scotland and England. His assessment was always in terms of social utility. Many punishments were accordingly judged excessive and the English laws of real property were often mischievous. He was severely critical of legal bequests in perpetuity.

> Upon the whole nothing can be more absurd than perpetual entails. In them the principle of testamentary succession can by no means take place. Piety to the dead can only take place when their memory is fresh in the minds of men: a power to dispose of estates for ever is manifestly absurd. . . . The utmost extent of entails should be those who are alive at the person's death, for he can have no affection to those who are unborn. Entails are disadvantageous to the improvement of the country,

and those lands where they have never taken place are always best cultivated: heirs of entailed estates have it not in their view to cultivate lands, and often they are not able to do it. A man who buys land has this entirely in view, and in general the new purchasers are the best cultivators. (*Lectures*, p. 124)

In the last section, on the subject of real legal rights, Smith dealt with those "creatures of the civil law," the monopolies and the privileges of corporations. As we should expect, these are roundly condemned: "When a number of butchers have the sole privilege of selling meat, they may agree to make the price what they please, and we must buy from them whether it be good or bad. Even this privilege is not of advantage to the butchers themselves, because the other trades are also formed in corporations and if they sell beef dear they must buy bread dear. But the great loss is to the public, to whom all things are rendered less comeatable, and all sorts of work worse done; towns are not well inhabited, and the suburbs are increased."[2]

CHAPTER VII

The Genesis of the Wealth of Nations

THE last section of Smith's Glasgow course opened under the heading "Of Police." This word, Smith told his listeners, originally derived from a Greek term which properly signified the *policy* of civil government. By the eighteenth century it had come to mean only the regulation of the "inferior parts" of government "such as viz: cleanliness, security and cheapness or plenty." Smith's lectures on cleanliness and security took up only two pages of notes. On the subject of "cheapness or plenty" (or what we would now call abundance or prosperity) his lectures expanded into a hundred pages. He had reached the province of the political economist and the threshold of his classical work.

In the lectures which followed there appeared material which could be described as *The Wealth of Nations* in draft. There were differences, however. For instance, the Lectures contain an opening section on consumption, a topic which is conspicuously (and many would say unfortunately) missing in the book. Previous to a consideration of the question

"wherein opulence consists," we must consider, argued
Smith, the "natural wants of mankind" which are to be supplied. Nature provided sufficiently for the animal kingdom;
but in contrast, "such is the delicacy of man alone" that no
object is produced to his liking; in everything there is need of
improvement. The industry of human life was employed not
merely in procuring the humble necessities of food and cloth-
ing ". . . but in procuring the conveniences of it according to
the nicety and and delicacy of our taste. To improve and
multiply the materials, which are the principal objects of our
necessities, gives occasion to all the variety of the arts." (*Lectures*, p. 160) Smith would not have been among those
gloomy twentieth-century prophets who foretold (and foretell) that after everybody has a full stomach, a car and a
house, capitalism would (will) grind to a halt for the want of
things to do. New supplies lead to new demands and vice
versa; investment opportunity does not wilt, its frontiers are
ever expanding. All this is clear in Smith who, of course, has
many disciples today. Consider for instance Frank Knight:
"The 'object' in the narrow sense of the present want is
provisional; it is as much a means to a new want as end to the
old one, and all intelligently conscious activity is directed
forward, onward, upward, indefinitely. Life is not fundamentally a striving for ends, for satisfaction, but rather for
bases for further striving; desire is more fundamental to
conduct than is achievement, or perhaps better, the true
achievement is the refinement and elevation of the plane of
desire, the cultivation of taste."[1]

Having determined that the end of social organization was
to provide for natural wants, Smith next sets about analyzing
the most appropriate means. As in *The Wealth of Nations*,
the feature of successful societies which receives predomi-

nant emphasis is the principle of the division of labor. Increased dexterity, a saving of time lost in passing "from one species of labour to another" and the invention and application of machinery—all followed from this principle. The famous pin factory example which later appears with enlargement in *The Wealth of Nations* is here set out in its essentials.

The lesson was driven home with vigor. The principles of good policy were asserted and reasserted. Then came a sudden body blow: the contrast with *false* principles; the declaration of war on the prevailing political economy of mercantilism. ". . . the division of labour is the great cause of the increase in public opulence, which is always proportioned to the industry of the people, and not to the quantity of gold and silver, as is foolishly imagined, . . . the industry of the people is always proportioned to the division of labour."

The lectures next proceeded with an examination of the "circumstances" which regulated the prices. Smith switched backwards and forwards between the concept of "natural price" and that of "market price." The "market price" received the more pungent support: "When a buyer comes to the market, he never asks of the seller what expenses he has been at in producing them." Smith sharply criticized public policy that caused prices to be higher than "normal." Government sponsorship of monopolies was a clear target. Another was taxation upon industry and, among other things, upon "leather, shoes, salt and beer or whatever is the strong drink of the country. . . ." (*Lectures*, p. 179)

> Man is an anxious animal, and must have his care swept off by something that can exhilarate the spirits. [Smith himself liked his wine.] It is alleged that this tax upon beer is an artificial security against drunkenness, but if we attend to it, we will

find that it by no means prevents it. In countries where strong liquors are cheap, as in France and Spain, the people are generally sober, but in northern countries, where they are dear, they do not get drunk with beer, but with spirituous liquors; nobody presses his friend to a glass of beer, unless he choose it. (*Lectures*, p. 179)

The anti-mercantilist theme was next renewed in a section on money. Under the proposition heading: "That Natural Opulence does not consist in Money," Smith argued that "the absurd opinion" that riches consisted in money had given rise to many "prejudicial errors in practice." One of these was the prohibition of the export of coin. Another, and more important, was the severe trade regulations to support the balance of trade.

Those species of commerce which drain us of our money are thought disadvantageous, and those which increase it beneficial, therefore the former are prohibited and the latter encouraged. As France is thought to produce more of the elegancies of life than this country, and as we take much from them, and they need little from us, the balance of trade is against us, and therefore almost all our trade with France is prohibited by the great taxes and duties in importation. On the other hand, as Spain and Portugal take more of our commodities than we of theirs, the balance is in our favour, and this trade is not only allowed, but encouraged. The absurdity of these regulations will appear on the least reflection. (*Lectures*, p. 204)

Then came the trump card, the one that Smith was to play over and over again: "All commerce that is carried on betwixt any two countries must necessarily be advantageous to both. The very intention of commerce is to exchange your own commodities for others which you think will be more convenient for you. When two men trade between themselves it is undoubtedly for the advantage of both. . . . The case is exactly the same betwixt any two nations." (*Lectures*, p. 204)

Another false mercantilist principle was that no public expense employed at home could be hurtful. People who inherited money and then disposed of the proceeds in riotous living reduced the capital of the country, argued Smith. Such practices could reduce the whole country "to the lowest pitch of misery." The lectures were clearly beginning to sizzle.

In view of the spectacular and visible advantages of the division of labor, why was it, demanded Smith, that every nation should continue so long "in a poor and indigent state"? First, no doubt, there were some impediments, such as bad climate or topography and ignorance among "rude and barbarous people" of the effects of the division of labor. Moreover, before labor could be divided, some accumulation of capital was necessary. In the beginnings of society it was particularly difficult to produce more than a bare subsistence ". . . 'til some stock be produced there can be no division of labour, and before the division of labour takes place there can be very little accumulation of stock." (*Lectures*, p. 223) In a nation of savages, furthermore, there was no efficient government to protect property rights. The people, finding themselves every moment in danger of being robbed of all they possessed, had no motive to be industrious. Even where the power of government was sufficient to defend the produce of industry another obstacle often arose "from a different quarter": the threat of hostile invasion, plunder and perpetual war. Under these circumstances, too, it was "next to impossible" that any accumulation of capital could be made.

But for vast areas of the world these explanations would not hold. Many countries were able to maintain domestic order and to resist invasion. What, then, was the main source of the trouble? There was only one answer: incompetent government. At this stage Smith's combative words leap out of the pages. Consider the items on his charge sheet: To begin with, governments tolerated inefficient legal structures. Antiquated systems of primogeniture and land tenure, burdensome taxes and unnecessary subsidies all undermined individual motives to improvement. Furthermore, privileged government sectors were often indifferent to the aim of increasing prosperity of their subjects. Moreover, in the few cases where active government interest was shown in the pursuit of public welfare, costly mistakes were made. Aristocrats and monarchs with their own presumptuous views as to the "proper" direction of industry and commerce developed into heavy-handed amateur planners, or in Smith's eighteenth-century terminology, "lovers of system." Some monarchs, for instance, deciding that agriculture was "the main-spring" of prosperity, gave to it special privileges which led to injury of other parts of the economy.

> Philip IV went to the plough himself in order to set the fashion. He did everything for the farmers except bringing them a good market; he conferred the titles of nobility on several farmers; he very absurdly endeavoured to oppress manufacturers with heavy taxes in order to force them to the country; he thought that in proportion as the inhabitants of towns became more numerous, those in the country decreased.

On the contrary, Smith argued, the greater the number of manufacturers in any country the more improved was its agriculture. "In England the country has been better stored with corn, and the price of it has gradually sunk, since the exportation of it was permitted." (*Lectures*, p. 230)

Smith was now in full sail. (How explosive these lectures must now have been!) There were many more broadsides to come. Governments had miserably failed to reform the law with regard to contracts. Moreover, the improvement of commerce was severely hindered by the difficulty of conveyance from one place to another. "In our own country a man made his testament before he set out from Edinburgh to Aberdeen, and it was still more dangerous to go to foreign countries." (*Lectures*, p. 234) Government support for, or creation of, monopolies, exclusive privileges of corporations and state-granted licences characteristically came in for Smith's severest condemnation. On the subject of the Statute of Apprentices: "It was imagined that the cause of so much bad cloth was that the weaver had not been properly educated, and therefore they made a statute that he should serve a seven years apprenticeship before he pretended to make any. But this is by no means a sufficient security against bad cloth. . . ." (*Lectures*, p. 236)

Smith next condemned inefficient taxation policy as another prominent hindrance to economic progress. Granted that governments required a certain minimum revenue, it was irresponsible of them to refuse careful consideration of the alternative methods of raising it. Smith examined the taxes under two divisions: taxes upon possessions (capital) and taxes upon consumption, and showed a strong leaning towards the former. Among possessions land was a better taxable item than stock in trade or money. Certainly the taxes upon land possessions had a great advantage over taxes on commodities. The costs of collecting the land tax of England were not more than ten thousand pounds, and the collectors were people with integrity, for were they not chosen by the "gentlemen of the country" who were obliged to produce proper security for their carrying safely to the Exchequer the money which they collect? In contrast, the taxes of customs and excise, although they produced immense sums, were almost eaten up by "legions of officers" that were employed in collecting them. Smith, of course, was here speaking from direct family experience. Customs officers, he reminded his audience, had to have supervisors over them to examine their proceedings. The supervisors in turn were subordinate to Collectors, who in their turn were under the Commissioners, who were accountable to the Exchequer. "To support these officers there must be levied a great deal more than the government requires, which is a manifest disadvantage." (*Lectures*, p. 241)

Such, then, was the developing style of the Glasgow Lectures on the great theme of the subsequent classical *Wealth of Nations*. Smith was no romantic or Utopian, that was clear. His awareness of the failings of his fellow men qualified his writing at every turn; not for him the naïve Enlightenment view that progress was *inevitable*. The division of labor could certainly do wonders if given the chance. However, where its development was not hindered by indirect obstacles it was otherwise thwarted by the follies of governments. Were even scholars and reformers helpless before them? Smith's own battle was obviously already on. If he was no believer in the inevitability of progress, neither was he convinced that there was inevitability in decay or stagnation. The stronger his own fulminations against bad governments, the more he demonstrated the implication of the possibility of their reform. If historians, philosophers and other scholars would only get down to their proper task of analyzing the true *causes*, "the dependencies and connections" of things, they could at least offer some sensible and practicable advice to which some statesmen somewhere might pay attention. Smith was certainly against "over-government"; but he was the last person to entertain the slightest notions of anarchy: "No government is quite perfect, but it is better to submit to some inconveniencies than make attempts against it." It was better still to work at removing the inconveniences:

> He is not a citizen who is not disposed to respect the laws and to obey the civil magistrate; and he is certainly not a good citizen who does not wish to promote, by every means in his power, the welfare of the whole society of his fellow-citizens.[2]

CHAPTER VIII

The Impartial Spectator

THE achievement and scholarship of the Glasgow Lectures on Rhetoric, Literary Style, Justice, Security and "Cheapness or Plenty" would have been enough for most men. Simultaneously, however, Smith was engaged on still another project, this time in connection with his lecture course on Ethics. In 1759 the fruits of prodigious work on this subject were published in his first book, *The Theory of Moral Sentiments*. Sensitive, original, erudite, eloquent and in language which Burke was to describe as "rather painting than writing," this was the work which first revealed to the world the full stature of Smith's genius. If *The Wealth of Nations* had never been written this previous work would have earned for him a prominent place in intellectual history. It is certainly unfortunate that the second book has overshadowed his first to the extent that it has. It will be the business of the present chapter to attempt to explain why. The review of this part of Smith's intellectual work in particular is undertaken in the belief that it especially affords valuable insight on his own tastes and personality. More conventional and direct biography will be resumed in the following chapter.

Long after his death Adam Smith's harshest critics began to quote him as the classical "apologist" of capitalism, the insensitive theoriser, the man who believed in the "survival of the fittest" in a world dominated by the cash-nexus and ruthless warlike competition. No writer was more responsible for the promulgation of this interpretation of Smith than Karl Marx. The following is an extract from his works:

> According to Adam Smith, *society* is a *commercial enterprise*. Every one of its members is a *salesman*. It is evident how political economy establishes an *alienated* form of social intercourse, as the *true and original* form, and that which corresponds to human nature.[1]
>
> The less you eat, drink and read books; the less you go to the theatre, the dance hall, the public-house; the less you think, love, theorize, sing, paint, fence, etc., the more you *save*—the *greater* becomes your treasure which neither moths nor rust will devour—*your capital*. The less you *are*, the more you *have*; the less you express your own life, the greater is your *externalized* life—the greater is the store of your alienated being. Everything that the political economist takes from you in life and in humanity, he replaces for you in *money* and in *wealth*; and all the things that you cannot do, your money can do.[2]

Such interpretations reveal the deficiencies not of Adam Smith but of his censors. Their mistakes arise partly from a careless reading of *The Wealth of Nations* and partly from a failure to realize that this book is only one component of a larger and more comprehensive investigation of man in society. A reading of *The Theory of Moral Sentiments* is essential if full perspective is to be attained.

It is true that much of Adam Smith's economics in *The Wealth of Nations* is based on one predominant assumption about human behavior: that in his material pursuits man obeys the dictates of self-interest. Indeed, it was more than an assumption in Smith's mind, it was boldly stated as a fact. Modern economists are much more tentative about conceding the operation of what has now come to be called the profit motive. So anxious are they to avoid being called materialists that they gingerly present "profit maximization" only as a tentative working hypothesis. In this attitude they consider themselves to be superior to what they think to be the cruder formulations of their classical ancestor. But why the guilt complex? Smith in fact was much more aware than most of his successors of the complex motives in human life. Where he confined himself to the role of the economist he remained fully conscious that he was concentrating only on one area of human behavior. There were many motives in life, some stronger than others, some more noble. In the ordinary business of getting a living, generalizations about human behavior required an assumption not about which motives were highest but which were strongest. Nobody knew more than Smith how exquisitely the higher motives were expressed elsewhere in life. His *total* work looks at man in *all* his dimensions.

In *The Wealth of Nations* he deals primarily with the strong motives; in *The Moral Sentiments* with the higher ones. What is it, he asks in the latter work, that prompts ordinary persons to be benevolent as well as self-interested, to be virtuous as well as mundane, to be humane as well as human? Smith the young Professor of Moral Philosophy settles into the task of reviewing, sifting and augmenting the philosophical works of his most influential predecessors. In one expansive volume he examines, or refers to, Plato, Aristotle, Epicurus, Zeno, Epictetus, Cicero, Grotius, Mandeville, Hobbes, Locke, David Hume and the most influential of all, Hutcheson. Here predominantly were the traditional Stoics and utilitarians. The latter had explained all virtue in terms of usefulness to the individual or to society. For instance, the virtuous pleasure we get from the fellow-feeling that accompanies our neighbors' approval of some of our actions was simply the reflection, argued Hume, of our pleasure in the knowledge that our neighbors are likely to help and protect us. It was this kind of reasoning which Smith also found in the works of Hobbes, Duffendorf and Mandeville; and it was this kind of position that he was anxious to challenge:

> Those who are fond of deducing all our sentiments from certain refinements of self-love, think themselves at no loss to account, according to their own principles, both for this pleasure and this pain. Man, say they, conscious of his own weakness, and of the need which he has for the assistance of others, rejoices whenever he observes that they adopt his own passions, because he is then assured of that assistance; and grieves whenever he observes the contrary because he is then assured of his opposition.[3]

This explanation was mistaken, Smith argued; "fellow-feeling" denotes man's *genuine* interest in the happiness of his neighbor; it is quite free from ulterior motive. True, he tells us in his later book, *The Wealth of Nations,* that it is not from benevolence that the butcher provides you with your dinner. But here, in effect, he tells us that it is not from self-interest that the butcher jumps into the river to save you from drowning. Self-interest lives side by side with benevolence. They are not incompatible; each has its part to play at the appropriate time; and exclusively to concentrate upon one dimension of life is seriously to distort the whole.

Dramatic acts of altruism such as the rescue of drowning neighbors are not the only manifestations of benevolence. Smith takes us through a whole subtle range of human relationships wherein human beings say or do things, not for the purpose of reward but because it is the "right" thing to do. But moral philosophy demands a unifying principle. Was there such a principle to which people referred before performing these "right" actions? If there was it had not yet been found, claimed Smith. There was an infinite number of real life situations; no one discovered "set of rules" could be adequate to cover each and every one. Wide scope for judgement, creativity and inspiration must accompany any quest for *the* comprehensive moral code.

Special assistance was available to us, however, if only we looked deeply enough. This assistance came to us via a certain agent, a "guiding light," which Smith calls the Impartial Spectator; and with it he offers his own original contribution to moral philosophy. This agency, as we shall see, is something akin to "conscience" or what he calls "the internal spectator" or "man within the breast." He is not content, however, to rest his case simply on some triumphant utterance of a single word or magic phrase. Instead he makes a serious attempt to go behind such terms as "conscience" in search of deeper meaning.

Smith rejects the idea put forward by his predecessors Shaftesbury and Hutcheson that every man is endowed by nature with an innate moral sense. It is more important, he tells us, to notice a certain propensity in men to "sympathize with" each other's emotion and to do so with a care and imagination which is both sincere and human. There is within us, claims Smith, a true-hearted desire to enter into or identify ourselves with the joys and sorrows of others. This desire in turn leads us to try to win and to keep the sympathy of others. Behavior prompted by such sympathy is at the root of all benevolent acts.

Start with a simple case of one person, call him the actor, who behaves in such a way as accidentally to bring misfortune upon himself. There is a second individual, the Spectator, who can be an imagined or real person, who has, says Smith, a propensity to enter into and share sorrows of the former. The actor, seeing that he is being sympathized with, then begins to regret being the cause of the evident distress in the Spectator. He next tries to improve the joint situation by a renewed attempt to control his own grief. By such reciprocal action the discrepancies in the intensity of the feelings between the two are gradually reduced. Such marginal adjustments eventually lead to a new emotional equilibrium, "a concord of feelings."

The Spectator, however, does not always "go along with" the actor's feelings. Consider a situation where feelings of anger, for instance, have provoked the actor into injuring a third party. The Spectator in this case has to judge between two persons, and normally, says Smith, he is predisposed against the provoked and towards the injured party. The finest distinctions of moral approbation or disapprobation now enter the picture; the Impartial Spectator of events, in his sympathy for the party affected, is now obliged to make more sophisticated judgements. The parties themselves, however, are predisposed to seek (in advance) the sympathy of the Spectator. This being so, they anticipate his judgement and modify their action almost before it has begun. Even if they do not identify any particular person as the chief Spectator they will "imagine" one "within the breast." In turn, the judgement of this imagined Impartial Spectator is measured by their own experience of being sympathizers, judges and spectators of the actions of others. With such "triangular" and reciprocal fellow-feeling Smith builds his system of moral philosophy.

It will be seen that the analysis is based upon the assumption that man is a social animal; without the society of his fellows the individual could have no "mirror" of his own actions.

> Were it possible that a human creature could grow up to manhood in some solitary place, without any communication with his own species, he could no more think of his own character, of the propriety or demerit of his own sentiments and conduct, of the beauty or deformity of his own mind, than of the beauty or deformity of his own face. All these are objects which he cannot easily see, which naturally he does not look at, and with regard to which he is provided with no mirror which can present them to his view. Bring him into society, and he is immediately provided with the mirror which he wanted before. It is placed in the countenance and behaviour of those he lives with, which always mark when they enter into, and when they disapprove of his sentiments; and it is here that he first views the propriety and impropriety of his own passions, and the beauty and deformity of his own mind. (*Moral Sentiments*, p. 162)

When such a person is brought into society not only is he

given a measure of the "propriety" of his own passions but he is led to readjust his life according to new motivations.

> Bring him into society, and all his own passions will immediately become the causes of new passions. He will observe that mankind approve of some of them, and are disgusted by others. He will be elevated in the one case, and cast down in the other; his desires and aversions, his joys and sorrows, will now often become the cause of new desires and new aversions, new joys and new sorrows: they will now, therefore, interest him deeply, and often call upon his most attentive consideration. (*Moral Sentiments*, p. 163)

The practice of living with one's fellows has the psychological result of moderating all the extremes of feeling. This desire for moderation, together with the notion that ethics is a function of social life, is clearly reminiscent of Aristotle. Whereas Aristotle presented the "golden mean" as an ideal to be striven for, Smith goes further and suggests that the mean will be reached *in fact*. The success is achieved by the convergence of feelings brought about by the silent agency of the Impartial Spectator's guidance of each member of society.

Smith's principle cannot be written off as mere conformity with public opinion. Man is motivated, certainly, by the search for approbation of his fellows; but he desires not only praise, but *praiseworthiness*, "or to be that thing which, though it should be praised by nobody, is, however, the natural and proper object of praise. He dreads, not only blame, but also blameworthiness; or to be that thing which, though it should be blamed by nobody, is, however, the natural and proper object of blame." (*Moral Sentiments*, p. 166) Smith observes that the most sincere praise can give us little pleasure when we know in our heart that we have not deserved it. We know that the man who applauds us for actions which we did not perform "applauds not us, but another person." Our anxious desire that we ourselves should excel is, says Smith, "originally founded in our admiration of the excellence of others." Neither can we be satisfied with being merely admired for what other people are admired. We must at least believe ourselves to be admirable for what they are admirable. In order to attain this satisfaction, however, we must become the Impartial Spectator of our *own* character and conduct. In other words, we are prompted by the desire not only of gaining the respect of others but also of gaining our own self-respect.

The Spectator sometimes makes mistakes. In the short run his judgement may be impeded by temporary excitements and fashionable enthusiasms. It is the quiet, retrospective judgements, Smith explains, which are the most reliable; and it is these that give us the best starting point for any search for a code of general rules or principles of conduct. If we persist in the search we should remember, he insists, that there could be no basis in mere deductive logic. "Codification" must be the patient outcome of innumerable generalizations, from experience, from a multitude of judgements and from the vast variety of circumstances that we encounter throughout life. The basis of the moral laws of nature therefore was certainly not some simple mechanical utilitarian ethic; morality grew out of an infinity of feelings, situations and intuitions. There may of course be some utilitarian consequences in the shape of material benefits accruing to individuals or to society; but these will usually be merely a by-product.

Marxists and others who link Smith's philosophy with some crude law of the jungle where only the "fittest" survive are thus sadly out of touch. In the nineteenth century a vigorous defense of Adam Smith was made, interestingly enough, by T. H. Huxley, one of the very founders of the biological concept of the "survival of the fittest." It was a fallacy to suppose, argued Huxley, that because the forces of nature in the biological world seemed insensible and deterministic, it was proper for humanity to simulate the "battle for survival" in "a natural, unsentimental" manner. Nature had several levels of existence and it was wrong to impute the rules of one level to that of another. The moral basis for human behavior was not to be discovered in any analogy with the mechanical workings of "non-human" life. In Huxley's view Adam Smith was correct to have sought for a basis of morality not in non-human but in *human* nature.[4]

What of the relationship between Smith's philosophy and his economics? Take the question of the human struggle against poverty and towards wealth. It is again interesting to examine Marx's interpretation of Smith and to compare the vision of each writer. In *Capital* Marx quotes from *The Wealth of Nations* Smith's sentence: "Industry furnishes the material which saving accumulates." Marx then "reads into" Adam Smith the following corollary:

> Therefore you must save, you must save; you must reconvert the largest possible proportion of surplus value or surplus product in capital. Accumulation for accumulation's sake, production for production's sake, this was the formula by which the classical political economists gave expression to the historical mission of the bourgeois period. They were under no illusions as to the labour pains at-

tendant upon the birth of wealth, but what is the
use of deploring historical necessity? . . . Accumulate! Accumulate! That is Moses and all the prophets.[5]

Now compare Adam Smith's infinitely more sophisticated
position. To what purpose, Smith asks, is all the toil and
bustle of this world?

> Is it to supply the necessities of nature? The wages
> of the meanest labourer can supply them. We say
> that they have bought him food and clothing, the
> comfort of a house, and of a family. If we examine
> his economy with rigour, we should find that he
> spends a great part of them upon conveniences,
> which may be regarded as superfluities, and that,
> upon extraordinary occasions, he can give some-
> thing even to vanity and distinction. What then is
> the cause of our aversion to this situation, and why
> should those who have been educated in the higher
> ranks of life, regard it as worse than death, to be
> reduced to live, even without labour, upon the
> same simple fare with him, to dwell under the
> same lowly roof, and to be clothed in the same
> humble attire? Do they imagine that their stomach
> is better, or their sleep sounder, in a palace than in
> a cottage? (*Moral Sentiments*, p. 70)

Smith answers that all this feverish economic activity is
prompted simply by mankind's desire to seek sympathy. Since
people sympathize more with our joy than with our sorrow
we try to conceal our poverty and to parade our riches. The
alleged deficiencies of the affluent society and the psychology
of "keeping up with the Jones's" are not new; they were all
examined long ago in Smith's survey of eighteenth-century

society. "It is the vanity, not the ease, or the pleasure, which interests us." The more riches a person had, the more attention he brought to himself. Though his neighbors might have envied him somewhat they also "put themselves in his place" and to this extent shared his joy of being such a center of attention.

This sympathy (or what we now call empathy) was of such intensity, indeed, that the downfall of the very wealthy was felt with vicarious grief by the mass of the population much more than the relative fall of more lowly persons. This fact is clearly reflected in poetry and drama. "It is the misfortunes of kings only which afford the proper subject for tragedy. They resemble, in this respect the misfortunes of lovers. . . . To disturb or put an end to, such perfect enjoyment, seems to be the most atrocious of all injuries. The traitor who conspires against the life of his monarch, is thought a greater monster than any other murderer. All the innocent blood that was shed in the civil wars, provoked less indignation than the death of Charles I." (*Moral Sentiments*, p. 73) It was upon this willingness of mankind "to go along with" many of the vicissitudes of the rich and the powerful that class divisions, or what Smith called "the distinction of ranks," were sustained. What a distance from Marxism!

> Our obsequiousness to our superiors more frequently arises from our admiration for the advantages of their situation, than from any private expectations of benefit from their good-will. Their benefits can extend but to a few; but their fortunes interest almost everybody. We are eager to assist them in completing a system of happiness that approaches so near to perfection; and we desire to serve them for their own sake, without any other

recompense but the vanity of the honour of oblig-
ing them. (*Moral Sentiments*, p. 73)

The Spectator's feelings for the rich, Smith maintains, arise
not so much because of the superior ease or pleasure which
they enjoy as of the "artificial and elegant contrivances" for
promoting this ease or pleasure. "He does not even imagine
that they are really happier than other people; but he imag-
ines that they possess more means of happiness. And it is the
ingenious and artful adjustment of those means to the end
for which they were intended, that is the principle source of
his admiration." (*Moral Sentiments*, p. 262) The motive
that prompts us to so much hard work is not so much the
necessity of meeting our basic physical requirements as the
human fascination with the workings of machines, gadgets
and "systems." We are almost obsessed with the way in which
the means of the rich man are so nicely, so fittingly, so exquisitely designed to achieve the ends. The devices which we
enjoy may in the end serve only trivial or frivolous purposes;
this does not matter. The "artful adjustment, the beauty of
the arrangement" matters most for it truly inspires us. He
gives the following charming illustration: our delight in
pocket watches.

A watch, . . . that falls behind above two minutes
in a day, is despised by one curious in watches. He
sells it perhaps for a couple of guineas, and purchases another at fifty, which will not lose above a
minute in a fortnight. The sole use of watches, however, is to tell us what o'clock it is, and to hinder us
from breaking any engagement, or suffering any
other inconveniency by our ignorance in that particular point. But the person so nice with regard to
this machine will not always be found either more

scrupulously punctual than other men, or more anxiously concerned upon any other account to know precisely what time of day it is. What interests him is not so much the attainment of this piece of knowledge, as the perfection of the machine which serves to attain it. (*Moral Sentiments*, p. 259)

Is most economic activity then nothing but a dissipation of men's energies? No, says Smith; such a view comes only from the weariness of old age and from the sour and prim critics of the affluent society.

Power and riches appear then (in old age) to be, what they are, enormous and operose machines contrived to produce a few trifling conveniences to the body, consisting of springs the most nice and delicate, which must be kept in order with the most anxious attention, and which, in spite of all our care, are ready every moment to burst into pieces, and to crush in their ruins their unfortunate possessor. (*Moral Sentiments*, p. 262)

This kind of view, this "splenetic philosophy," accompanies sickness and low spirits as well as old age. When in good health and humor we have a much more agreeable outlook. Our imagination then "expands itself to everything around us." And it is well, continues Smith, that we are naturally disposed in our healthful state to be actively absorbed to the point of obsession. For economic and cultural reasons the pursuit of wealth is "a necessary deception." "It is this deception which rouses and keeps in continual motion the industry of mankind. It is this which first prompted them to cultivate the ground, to build houses, to found cities and commonwealth. . . . The earth, by these labours of mankind, has been obliged to redouble her natural fertility, and to maintain a greater multitude of inhabitants." (*Moral Sentiments*, p. 263) It is because of a particular psychology of man that investment opportunities are continually being opened and fruitful ideas stimulated. Unlike Marx, Smith asserts that the effect of all this is to spread prosperity all down the social scale. Even if a "proud and unfeeling" landlord surveys his "extensive fields" without a thought for the wants of his brethren, the wealth of the latter proceeds in parallel with that of the former. The capacity of the landlord's stomach "bears no proportion to the immensity of his desires, and will receive no more than that of the meanest peasant."

> The rich only select from the heap what is most precious and agreeable. They consume little more than the poor. . . . (*Moral Sentiments*, p. 264) In ease of body and peace of mind, all the different ranks of life are nearly upon a level, and the beggar, who suns himself by the side of the highway, possesses that security which kings are fighting for. (*Moral Sentiments*, p. 265)

If this was the *economic* explanation, what of the *cultural* reason why the pursuit of wealth was a "necessary deception"? Smith's answer was quite uncomplicated. The very acts of perfecting devices and of inventing associated with the creation of wealth simply led to the improvement of the sciences and the arts, and these "ennoble and embellish human life."

On the sociology of capitalism Marx and Smith were poles apart. In Marx's view, capitalism caused the ordinary individual to be poor, dehumanized and alienated. For Smith, capitalism (provided there was freedom) helped him become affluent, "humanized" and *un*alienated.[6]

Smith's Impartial Spectator was not content merely to see

mankind feed itself; he wanted it to display "generous, noble or tender sentiments" and to enjoy active, inquisitive and inventive minds. He wanted man (and man wanted himself) to achieve a balance between the separate aspects of his life. Smith was very sensitive to the danger that human folly would lead to an imbalance. Men could easily become overabsorbed in their striving for novelties as a means of winning sympathy. Obsessive admiration for wealth was in the end "the great and universal cause of the corruption of our moral sentiments." Strict virtue demanded a sense of perspective and the exercise of proper restraint. Man did not live by bread alone; but neither did he live by "beneficence" alone. In striving to achieve a balance he became involved in the three simultaneous pursuits of "prudence, of strict justice, and of proper benevolence."

These deserve separate examination. Prudence was concerned with the achievement of the necessary conditions for preservation. It was perfectly right that the individual should look after his own body; this was not a selfish act in the pejorative sense of that word. "Thus, to give a very low instance, to eat when we are hungry, is certainly, upon ordinary occasions, perfectly right and proper, and cannot miss being approved of as such by everybody." Stories may be received from travellers that famine in those foreign parts was widespread. A person may properly display some anguish at the news (which may or may not be perfectly true). It would be going beyond the bounds of common sensibility, however, to starve himself on that account. "As to love our neighbour as we love ourselves is the great law of Christianity so it is the great precept of nature to love ourselves only as we love our neighbour, or, what comes to the same thing, as our neighbour is capable of loving us." (*Moral Sentiments*, p. 28) There is a problem in identifying the practical boundaries which en-

compass those we would call our "neighbours," those we are
duty bound to love; but common sense dictated that such an
attempt be made. As in the activity of feeding ourselves, so in
the process of saving and the creation of capital we are following the dictates of prudence. Accumulate? Prudence, although a necessary guide, is not a sufficient one. It is not one
of the "most endearing, or of the most ennobling of the virtues.
It commands a certain cold esteem, but seems not entitled to
any very ardent love or admiration." (*Moral Sentiments*, p.
316)

Next to Prudence comes Justice. By this Smith means the
observance of a set of legal rules by which each person's freedom is reasonably secured; by which, in other words, coer-
cion is outlawed. Justice, therefore, unlike prudence and
beneficence, is implemented by authority; it is the area of the
creation and observance of man-made laws. But again, Justice, like Prudence, provides a necessary, but not a sufficient,
condition for the achievement of full virtue in mankind. The
remaining requirement is what Smith calls "Beneficence."

Like Prudence, Beneficence refers to behavior that is vol-
untary and discretionary; without its free exercise man is not
complete. Beneficence is "an ornament which embellishes,
not the foundation which supports the building." Justice is,
upon most occasions, "but a negative virtue, and only hinders
us from hurting out neighbour." (*Moral Sentiments*, p. 117)
On the other hand, "Beneficence is always free, it cannot be
extorted by force, the mere want of it exposes us to no pun-
ishment; because the mere want of Beneficence tends to do
no real positive evil." But the Impartial Spectator is just as
disappointed, just as unsympathetic, when any individual
demonstrates a lack of Beneficence. The disapproval, of
course, is in a different category from that associated with an

act of injustice such as physical injury. While prudence may be the strongest motive of behavior, Beneficence is the highest: ". . . to feel much for others, and little for ourselves, . . . to restrain our selfish, and to indulge our benevolent, affections constitute the perfection of human nature; and can alone produce among mankind that harmony of sentiments and passions in which consists their whole grace and propriety."[7]

The Impartial Spectator is inside each of us and he is there to speak both for himself and for others. "Everyman is, no doubt, by nature, first and principally recommended to his own care; and as he is fitter to take care of himself, than of any other person, it is fit and right that it should be so." (*Moral Sentiments,* p. 119) Although the ruin of our neighbor may affect us much less than a small misfortune of our own, we must not, argues Smith, ruin our neighbor to prevent such a small personal misfortune. *"Nor even to prevent our own ruin."* We must here, as in all other cases, "view ourselves not so much according to that light in which we may naturally appear to ourselves, as according to that in which we naturally appear to others." (*Moral Sentiments,* p. 119) Although there may be a tendency for every individual to prefer himself to others, "yet he dares not look mankind in the face, and avow that he acts according to this principle. He feels that in this preference they can never go along with him, and that how natural soever it may be to him, it must always appear excessive and extravagant to them." (*Moral Sentiments,* p. 120) In the "race for wealth" the individual may run as hard as he can and strain every nerve and every muscle in order to get ahead but if he should use unfair means to throw down any of the competitors he will lose the indulgence of the Impartial Spectator. "It is a violation of fair play, which they cannot admit of." If one man does in-

jure another in the ordinary competition of life the Spectator's sympathy will go first to the injured.

The pursuit of justice, we have seen, consists of the setting
up of minimum rules which make more formal restraints on
self-interest in order to protect one person from harming another. In this case Smith acknowledges that the task of the
Spectator is particularly complicated and demanding; for to
achieve the best social consensus calls for the greatest wisdom
and reflection. His system now points to the political need for
some exceptional "scientific" legislator; but he shows himself
to be fully aware of the difficulties of recruiting such persons
from among fallible human beings. All things are possible,
however. The leader of a successful political party, he tells us,
may sometimes be of service to his country in a much more
important way than achieving foreign conquests. "He may re-
establish and improve the constitution, and from the very
doubtful and ambiguous character of the leader of a party, he
may assume the greatest and noblest of all characters, that of
the reformer and legislator of a great state; and, by the wisdom of his institutions, secure the internal tranquility and
happiness of his fellow-citizens for many succeeding generations." (*Moral Sentiments*, p. 341) But all this presupposes
that such a person "has authority enough to prevail upon his
own friends to act with proper temper and moderation
(which he frequently has not) . . ." (*Moral Sentiments*, p.
340) It is clear that in Smith's view the ideal legislator
should be strongly endowed with beneficence, or what he
calls in the political context, a "public spirit," a quality
which, however, so often becomes swamped by others.

The danger is that man's natural obsession with the nice-
ties of mechanical contrivances and his love of mechanisms
for their own sake will frustrate or sidetrack his public spirit.

The "spirit of system" was apt to compete with public spirit, which par excellence was founded "upon the love of humanity, upon a real fellow feeling. . . ." The "spirit of system" was the insatiable desire of the planner to construct society like a machine.

> This system commonly takes the direction of that more gentle public spirit, always animates it, and often inflames it, even to the madness of fanaticism. . . . The great body of the party are commonly intoxicated with the imaginary beauty of this ideal system, of which they have no experience, but which has been represented to them in all the most dazzling colours in which the eloquence of their leaders could paint it. Those leaders themselves, though they originally may have meant nothing but their own aggrandisement, become, many of them in time, the dupes of their own sophistry, and are as eager for this great reformation as the weakest and foolest of their followers. Even though the leaders should have preserved their own heads, as, indeed, they commonly do, free from this fanaticism, yet they dare not always disappoint the expectation of their followers, but are often obliged, though contrary to their principle and their conscience, to act as if they were under the common delusion.

By demanding too much, the governing party frequently obtained nothing, and the inconveniences and distresses were left "without the hope of remedy." The man whose public spirit was not so tainted, but was prompted by true benevolence, will act with tactful diplomacy and go along with some of the imperfect constructions of society, "moderating what he often cannot annihilate without great violence." "He will accommodate, as well as he can, his public arrangements to the confirmed habits and prejudices of the people, and will remedy, as well as he can, the inconveniences which may flow from the want of those regulations which the people are averse to submit to." (*Moral Sentiments*, p. 342) The "man of system," in contrast, was "wise in his own conceit."

> . . . he seems to imagine that he can arrange the different members of a great society with as much ease as the hand arranges the different pieces upon a chess-board; he does not consider that the pieces upon the chess-board have no other principle of motion besides that which the hand impresses upon them; but that, in the great chess-board of human society, every single piece has a principle of motion of its own, altogether different from that which the legislator might choose to impress upon it. (*Moral Sentiments*, p. 343)

Some planning, some erection of rules of justice, was of course necessary. And some element of vision of perfect policy and law was helpful. But to make impatient clamor to establish it all at once was to display the highest degree of arrogance.

> It is to erect his own judgement into the supreme standard of right and wrong. It is to fancy himself the only wise and worthy man in the commonwealth, and that his fellow-citizens should accommodate themselves to him, and not he to them.

Although no believer in the inevitability of progress, Smith did, in the end, display some measure of optimism. The pieces of the chess-board moved according to the principle of self-direction and also the principle of the pressure of the planner's hand.

> . . . if those two principles coincide and act in the
> same direction, the game of human society will go
> on easily and harmoniously, and is very likely to be
> happy and successful. If they are opposite or different, the game will go on miserably, and the
> society must be at all times in the highest degree of
> disorder. (*Moral Sentiments*, p. 343)

One final word needs to be said concerning Adam Smith's Impartial Spectator. Prompted by "public spirit," benevolence and genuine fellow-feeling, the Spectator, in his supreme moments, experienced elements of divine inspiration. In his fullest development of his concept, Smith reveals himself clearly as a religious man:

> This universal benevolence, how noble and generous so ever, can be the source of no solid happiness
> to any man who is not thoroughly convinced that
> all the inhabitants of the universe, the meanest as
> well as the greatest, are under the immediate care
> and protection of that great, benevolent, and allwise Being, who directs all the movements of nature, and who is determined, by his own unalterable perfections, to maintain in it at all times the
> greatest possible quantity of happiness. To this
> universal benevolence, on the contrary, the very
> suspicion of a fatherless world must be the most
> melancholy of all reflections; from the thought that
> all the unknown regions of infinite and incomprehensible space may be filled with nothing but endless misery and wretchedness.

Smith sees his wise and virtuous statesman, however, mainly as a partner of God—not a passive, fatalistic and awe-struck contemplator of the wider universe, hoping for divine guidance at every turn. The statesman has important things to do. He is allotted, after all, the care of his own happiness, and that of his family, his friends and his country. The fact that he is occupied in completing the more sublime "can never be an excuse for neglecting the more humble department." He must avoid charges similar to those made against Marcus Antonius, "that while he employed himself in philosophical speculations, and contemplated the prosperity of the universe, he neglected that of the Roman Empire." (*Moral Sentiments*, p. 348)

Several writers have been at pains to urge that the *Moral Sentiments* is primarily the work of an "optimistic theist," an advocate of the view that society is led by an "invisible hand" and into a state of "natural harmony." Smith's argument is indeed continually linked with references to the ordering of a supra-natural authority which he describes as "the Author of nature," "Nature," "The Conductor of the Universe," "Providence," and "the Deity." Nevertheless, we offer the opinion that the sympathy/spectator argument predominates in the *Moral Sentiments* and can be received as a self-sufficient excursion into moral philosophy. We suggest, too, that in the development of his theme much of the argument from "Deistic design" becomes a parallel and separate issue.[8]

Smith's *Moral Sentiments*, in fact, is a unique and tantalizing combination of philosophy, sociology, politics and theology. Theological and scientific processes of thought have, in the twentieth century, come to have more similarities in outlook than was once thought possible. It has recently been observed, for instance, that modern scientific activity "is analogous to the continual filling in and expansion of a gigantic jigsaw puzzle. No single scientist need know what the 'final' picture may look like, and the prevailing interpretation of the big picture may change progressively through time."[9] Scientific progress consequently consists in the search for an intuitive perception of relevant shapes or patterns. From this it follows that the scientist "explorer" postulates in advance some final concept of reality. "In science, man becomes as God in his vision of the natural universe."[10] Adam Smith's "theological" passages in the *Moral Sentiments* are often very reminiscent of this same sort of exploration. Terms such as Nature, Providence, and Infinite Wisdom are indeed sometimes presented with all the circumspection of working hypotheses. Yet Smith does clearly express the need through some sort of faith to direct one's private behavior towards God's wishes, "to co-operate with the Deity, and to advance as far as in our power the plan of Providence." As mortals, however, we can at most only see part of this plan; and although we are impressed with what appears to be serious imperfections in it on earth, we must believe in full reconciliation in the next world. Smith's concept of harmony in fact straddles this world and the next; it is for this reason that the fuller statement of the work of the Invisible Hand appears in the *Moral Sentiments* rather than in the later *Wealth of Nations*, which deals only with the economic aspects of life—an area which abounds in "untidiness" and "imperfections."[11]

On what basis do we on earth begin to try to cooperate with the Deity in fulfilling his plan? We do it, Smith asserts, through the exercise of our reasoning and feeling as reflected through the medium of the Impartial Spectator. It is apparent, however, that when Smith gets down to an examination of this same reasoning and feeling, he produces pieces of inductive or "practical" analysis which can appeal as self-sufficient to many who would reject his complementary theology. After much deliberation, assertion and speculation on the level of the supra-natural, Smith pronounces that "The administration of the great system of the universe, however, the care of the universal happiness of all rational and sensible beings, is the business of God and not of man. To man is allotted a much humbler department, but one much more suitable to the weakness of his powers, and to the narrowness of his comprehension; the care of his own happiness, of that of his family, his country . . ."[12] This "humbler department" which was for man "more suitable to the weakness of his powers" consisted largely of reason and "speculation." Again, in Chapter VI of Part III he examines openly whether religious principles should be regarded as the only proper motive of action. Should we only do things because God has commanded them? Smith characteristically replies that while it is the first precept of Christianity to love the Lord our God with all our heart it is the second to love our neighbor as ourselves; ". . . and we love ourselves surely for our own sakes, and not merely because we are commanded to do so." Philosophy and common sense had therefore an important and independent part to play. The subsequent inductive nature of Smith's own moral philosophy and its qualification to be considered in its own right has already been indicated. Consider next the development in Smith of another line of thought, which also seems to cut itself loose and to begin to stand on its own feet: his emerging political theory.

As we have already seen, one of the most important tasks for man's own intellect, according to Smith, was to devise a set of rules, a "system of justice," upon which mankind could live in concord. Men could not passively rely on some invisible hand to do this, they had to do it consciously for themselves. Smith did not entertain that kind of conservative political philosophy which believes that constitutions appear by some mystical process. True, we often respect those that we inherit; but the respect is directed not so much at Nature as at the accumulated wisdom of our predecessors. The ability, rationally, to improve constitutional rules was the quality which characterized the great statesman; the "greatest and noblest of all characters" was after all that of "the reformer and legislator of a great state."

In examining this process of constitution-building Smith almost stumbles upon important positive, as distinct from normative, propositions. For instance, in Part II, Chapter II, he starts with the Greek-like assertion that man can subsist happily only in society and that this will flourish where love, friendship and gratitude prevail. Smith then leads himself into the consideration of whether a society could subsist even without these positive virtues and concludes that it could. "Society may subsist among *different* men as among different merchants, from a sense of its utility, without any mutual love or affection; and though no man in it should owe any obligation, or be bound in gratitude to any other, it may still be upheld by a mercenary exchange of good offices according to an agreed valuation."[13] (Italics added) Smith was not saying that society can subsist among those who are ready to hurt each other; only that positive mutual affection is not a necessary condition. "If there is any society among robbers and murderers, they must at least, according to the trite observation, abstain from robbery and murdering one another."[14] This peculiarly Smithian departure from his inherited Greek traditions of thought is the emerging political analogue of his mutual-benefit-by-exchange theme of his "self-interest" economics. By such "calculus of consent" argument Smith reveals his grasp of a truth which is not theological or even scientific, but essentially political.[15] Politics, in the functional or constitutional sense, as distinct from the Greek idealist sense, is about consensus, not about visions of the "complete jigsaw" of a virtuously perfect and comprehensive state.[16] A constitution can be expected to emerge, Smith now argues, whose function it is simply to allow the coexistence of heterogeneous people. In the "great chess board of human society," Smith tells us, "every single piece *has a principle motion of its own*" (italics added).

Whether a constitution which contains such an individualistic society may possibly be consistent in the theologian's mind, as it seems to have been in Smith's, with the idea of a total unified picture visible only to God, will, for many people, be a matter for the theologian himself. The interesting fact meanwhile is that skeptics can accept the proposition as it stands shorn of any Deistic implications. For they will acknowledge as many "worlds" in a given legal constitution as there are individual members in it; such a constitution, in other words, is seen by the skeptic not as *the* good society but simply as a mechanism for tolerant interaction of almost as many "good societies" as there are individuals or groups within it.

Although certainly somewhat spasmodic, the above quotations of Smith do suggest that his thought was moving in this politically individualistic direction, a direction which was in some conflict with the Platonic and Stoic background in which he was nurtured. Smith, the believer in "natural liberty," was clearly beginning to acknowledge a kind of pragmatic negative liberty which sees politics, in the constitution-making sense, as an attempt to reach compromise between individuals with admittedly different values. He had arrived, in other words, at the threshold of the open society.

CHAPTER IX

The Glasgow Environment

IN 1759, the year of the publication of *The Theory of Moral Sentiments*, Smith, now 36 years old, was in the seventh year of his professorship at Glasgow. We have the evidence from a letter from David Hume, now a firmly established friend of Smith, of the way in which the book almost immediately established a reputation for him in learned circles well beyond the bounds of his own university. Writing to thank Smith for "the agreeable present" of some copies, Hume observed:

> Wedderburn and I made presents of our copies to such of our acquaintances as we thought good judges and proper to spread the reputation of the book. I sent one to the Duke of Argyle and Lord Lyttelton, Horace Walpole, Soame Jenyns and Burke, an English gentleman who wrote lately a very pretty treatise on the Sublime. Millar [the publisher] desired my permission to send one in your name to Dr. Warburton.

Hume proceeded in the letter to tease Smith by holding him

in suspense about the reception of the book. After several
digressions he continued:

My dear, but what is all this to my book, say you?
My dear Mr. Smith, have patience; compose yourself to tranquility. Show yourself a philosopher in
practice as well as profession. . . .

A wise man's kingdom is his own heart; or, if he
ever looks farther, it will only be to the judgement
of a select few, who are free from prejudices and
capable of examining his work. Nothing, indeed,
can be a stronger presumption of falsehood than
the approbation of the multitude; and Phocion,
you know, always suspected himself of some blun-
der when he was attended with the applause of the
populace.

Supposing, therefore, that you have duly prepared yourself for the worst by all these reflections,
I proceed to tell you the melancholy news that
your book has been very unfortunate, for the public seem disposed to applaud it extremely. It was
looked for by the foolish people with some impa-
tience; and the mob of literati are beginning to be
very loud in its praise. Three bishops called yester-
day at Millar's shop in order to buy copies, and to
ask questions about the author. The Bishop of
Peterborough said he had passed the evening in a
company where he heard it extolled above all
books in the world. . . . Lord Lyttelton says that
Robertson and Smith and Bower are the glories of
English literature . . . Millar exults and brags that
two-thirds of the edition are already sold, and that
he is now sure of success. You see what a son of the
earth that is, to value books only by the profit they
bring him. In that view, I believe, it may prove a
very good book.

The next paragraph of Hume's letter was later to be of much consequence in Smith's life:

> Charles Townshend, who passes for the cleverest fellow in England, is so much taken with the performance that he said to Oswald he would put the Duke of Buccleugh under the author's care, and would make it worth his while to accept of that charge. As soon as I heard this I called on him twice with the view of talking with him about the matter, and of convincing him of the propriety of sending that young gentleman to Glasgow, for I could not hope that he could offer you any terms which would tempt you to renounce your professorship; but I missed him.

A second letter on the same subject was written on the 28th of July from London:

> I am very well acquainted with Burke [Edmund Burke] who was much taken with your book. He got your direction from me with a view to writing to you and thanking you for the present, for I made it pass in your name. I wonder he has not done it. He is now in Ireland. I am not acquainted with Jenyns, but he spoke very highly of the book to Oswald, who is his brother in the Board of Trade. Millar showed me a few days ago a letter from Lord Fitzmaurice[1] where he tells him that he has carried over a few copies to the Hague for presents. Mr. York was very much taken with it, as well as several others who had read it.

In due course Smith's book received an adulatory review by Burke in *The Annual Register*. "The author," wrote

Burke, "seeks for the foundation of the just, the fit, the proper, the decent, in our most common and most allowed passions, and making approbation and disapprobation the tests of virtue and vice, and showing that these are founded on sympathy, he raises from the simple truth one of the most beautiful fabrics of moral theory that has perhaps ever appeared. The illustrations are numerous and happy, and show the author to be a man of uncommon observation. His language is easy and spirited, and puts things before you in the fullest light; it is rather painting than writing."

In Glasgow in the 1760's Smith's company was increasingly sought by many distinguished colleagues and acquaintances. Besides his successful authorship his reputation as a teacher was, according to Rae, so immense that "it was felt that another and perhaps greater Hutcheson had risen in the college." Visitors to Glasgow were impressed by the "great spirit of inquiry abroad among the young people in that city." Smith's opinions had also become the subjects of general discussion in the commercial parts of the city. The sons of the wealthier citizens used to go to College to take his class though they had no intention of completing a university course; stucco busts of him appeared in the book sellers' windows; "the very peculiarities of his voice and pronunciation received the homage of imitation."

What of his personality and style in the lecture room? We may be assured at least that he continued Hutcheson's innovation of lecturing in English and that he lectured "without books"! Smith evidently took his job very seriously; but not so seriously as to be a bore. One of his students, James Millar, gives us this description:

There was no situation in which the abilities of

Mr. Smith appeared to greater advantage than as a professor. In delivering his lectures he trusted almost entirely to extemporary elocution. His manner, though not graceful, was plain and unaffected, and as he seemed to be always interested in the subject, he never failed to interest his hearers. Each discourse consisted commonly of several distinct propositions, which he successively endeavoured to prove and illustrate. These propositions when announced in general terms had, from their extent, not unfrequently something of the air of paradox. In his attempts to explain them he often appeared at first not to be sufficiently possessed of the subject, and spoke with some hesitation. As he advanced, however, his manner became warm and animated, and his expression easy and fluent. On points susceptible of controversy you could easily discern that he secretly conceived an opposition to his opinions, and that he was led upon this account to support them with greater energy and vehemence. By the fullness and variety of his illustrations the subject gradually swelled in his hands and acquired a dimension which, without a tedious repetition of the same views, was calculated to seize the attention of his audience, and to afford them pleasure as well as instruction in following the same subject through all the diversity of shades and aspects in which it was presented, and afterwards in tracing it backwards to that original proposition or general truth from which this beautiful train of speculation had proceeded.[2]

In the last years of his life Smith was to look back upon his early years of teaching at Glasgow and to describe them as the happiest in all his experience. And there is no doubt that here was the academic professor par excellence. If he was primarily a scholar with the desire to publish, the writer in him was fundamentally dependent on the need to test his work and to experiment verbally before a critical young audience. If, alternatively, we see him primarily as a teacher, we observe the scholar close behind. As the dedicated teacher develops by making continual efforts at improving and perfecting his performance, so too does the man of letters. Smith gives his own clues:

> To impose upon any man the necessity of teaching, year after year, any particular branch of science, seems, in reality, to be the most effectual method for rendering him completely master of it himself. By being obliged to go every year over the same ground, if he is good for anything he necessarily becomes, in a few years, well acquainted with every part of it: and if upon any particular point he should form too hasty an opinion one year, when he comes in the course of his lectures to reconsider the same subject the year thereafter, he is very likely to correct it. As to be a teacher of science is certainly the natural employment of a mere man of letters, so is it likewise perhaps the education which is most likely to render him a man of solid learning and knowledge.[3]

A further instance of his pedagogic zeal is given to us by another student, who was told by Smith himself in his later life: "During one whole session, a certain student with a plain but expressive countenance was of great use to me in judging of my success. He sat conspicuously in front of a pillar: I had him constantly under my eye. If he leant forward to listen all was right, and I knew that I had the ear of my class; but if he leant back in an attitude of listlessness I felt at once that all was wrong, that I must change either the sub-ject or the style of my address."[4]

One of his students in 1760 was James Boswell. Writing to a friend in that year, Boswell shows rapturous praise:

> My greatest inducement for coming hither, was to hear Mr. Smith's lectures which are truly excellent. His Sentiments are striking, profound and beauti-full, the method in which they are arranged clear, accurate and orderly, his language correct perspic-uous and elegantly phrased. His private character is realy amiable. He has nothing of that formal stiffness and Pedantry which is too often found in Professors. So far from that, he is a most polite well-bred man, is extreamly fond of having his Stu-dents with him and treats them with all the easiness and affability imaginable.[5]

Evidence of his absence of mind reappears throughout Smith's life. His period as lecturer in Glasgow is no excep-tion. In the recently discovered lectures on literary style, the student reporter, faithfully writing down his teacher's verbal reference to an absent-minded character in history, makes a parenthetic note in Latin to the effect: "Listen who'se talk-ing!" Smith was well noted for this particular eccentricity in the several clubs to which he belonged while at Glasgow. At the Glasgow Dining Club, presided over by Smith's respected teacher of Mathematics, Professor Simson, it is reported that during the game of cards (which always followed a one-course dinner of chicken broth with a tankard of claret) Smith was a particularly bad partner. If an idea came to him in the middle of a game, so we are informed, he would "re-nounce or neglect to call."

It is interesting to notice that two of the younger men who

were members of Professor Simson's club were Joseph Black, the discoverer of latent heat, and James Watt, of steam engine fame. Watt has recorded that he owed much stimulus to the discussions of the club, which covered morality, literature and religion, "subjects in which they were all my superiors, I never having attended a college, and being then but a mechanic." Rae observes that it was another sign of the liberal spirit among the Glasgow professors that they should welcome "on a footing of perfect equality one who," as he says, "was then only a mechanic, but whose mental work they had the sense to recognise." Watt had come to Glasgow from London in 1756 and found that the close corporation of hammermen refused to allow him to set up as mechanic in the town. Smith and his Glasgow colleagues allowed him to set up a work shop and a sale room within the University precincts. It is ironic that Smith—who on all accounts never really predicted, or even noticed the birth of the Industrial Revolution—should have thus helped to nurture one of its most renowned engineers.

A more formal club that Smith belonged to was the Glasgow Literary Society, which had been founded in 1752. In 1753 he presented to it his review of David Hume's "Essays on Commerce." The level of discussion and debate was usually high and legend has it that on one occasion Smith engaged in a strenuous discussion on some subject for a whole evening against the entire assembly, and having lost his point by an overwhelming majority, was overheard muttering to himself, "convicted but not convinced."[6]

The economist also continued flourishing memberships with certain clubs in Edinburgh, even though the 44-mile journey by stage coach in those days took as long as thirteen hours. There he would visit his friend David Hume in his office of Librarian to the Faculty of Advocates and in his apartments in the Canongate, where he was writing his famous *History of England*. In Edinburgh too was his old friend James Oswald, now in an appointment at the Board of Trade.

Established on the lines of the French academies which James Oswald and Alan Ramsey had been impressed with in their Continental tour in 1739, the Edinburgh Select Society was indeed a novelty. Besides organizing discussions and debates it seriously undertook the task of promoting the arts, sciences and manufactures of Scotland. At its opening meeting Smith was responsible for explaining the objects of the new institution to the newly appointed and distinguished members. Membership eventually included Lord Kames, Robertson, Ferguson, Carlyle, Wallace (one of the instigators of the later Malthusian debate), Lauderdale, John Adam the celebrated architect, Dr. Cullen the distinguished medical professor, the statesman Charles Townshend, and the banker and Member of Parliament for the City, John Coutts. In 1775 Hume wrote in one of his letters that the Select Society had grown to be a national concern.

> Young and old, noble and ignoble, witty and dull, laity and clergy, all the world are ambitious of a place amongst us, and on each occasion we are as much solicited by candidates as if we were to choose a member of parliament. . . . The long drawling speakers have found out their want of talents and rise seldomer. In short, the House of Commons is less the object of general curiosity to London than the Select Society is to Edinburgh.[7]

Among the topics discussed by this Society were such questions as: Whether bounties on the exportation of corn be advantageous to trade and manufactures as well as to agriculture? Whether great or small farms are most advantageous to the country? What are the advantages and disadvantages of gentlemen of estates being farmers? What is the best and most proper duration of leases of land in Scotland? What proportion of the produce of lands should be paid as rent to the master? In what circumstances the rents of lands should be paid in money? In what kind? And in what time they should be paid? What is the best method of getting public highways made and repaired, whether by a turnpike law, as in many places in Great Britain, by country or parish work, by a tax, or by what other method? A record of these questions is preserved in the minutes of the Society, which exist today. Among other subjects discussed were outdoor relief, entail, banking, whisky duties, foundling hospitals, whether the institution of slavery be advantageous to the free and whether a union with Ireland would be advantageous to Great Britain.[8]

Taking in earnest its task of promoting the welfare of Scotland, the club set about establishing schemes of private incentives to the culture and economic life of the region. Following the foreign academies, it offered prizes and "public marks of distinction" for meritorious work in the arts, sciences and invention. Modern advocates of "balanced growth" will be intrigued to learn that before governments entertained such responsibilities these private bodies had a similar ambition. Observing that the art of printing in Scotland needed no encouragement in the 1750's, the prospectus of the Select Club was concerned because Scotland was not adequately providing the country with its own domestically manufactured paper. Suitable incentives were accordingly devised. Prizes were awarded for the excellence of workmanship in Scotch worsted, carpet making, whisky distilling and "the best drawings by boys or girls under sixteen years of age." This aspect of the committee's work went from strength to strength as monetary subscriptions from the nobles and aristocratic farmers poured in. The lists of industries needing stimulus increased and eventually included those of soap, cheese, gloves and hats. Even that modern symbol of "social costs," the smoking chimney, was under surveillance. Eventually it was announced that a premium was to be offered to the person who would "cure the greatest number of smokey chimneys to the satisfaction of the Society."

Outside the University, in addition to Smith's friends among the Scottish lawyer lairds, there were the businessmen acquaintances such as Andrew Cochrane, John Glassford, Colin Dunlop and John Gibson. It is generally agreed that the merchants of Edinburgh were less open to the ideas of free trade than were the merchants of Glasgow. "The Edinburgh merchants and bankers did not accept the ideas of Hume and Smith about the folly of trying to stop bullion outflows from Scotland, but behaved in the most mercantilist way possible, using all means in their power, including the refusal of credits, to stop this automatic adjustment from taking place through the export of coin and bullion. Once the Bank of Scotland and the Royal Bank of Scotland had resolved their difficulties with one another they formed a common front against Glasgow innovators by seeking a joint Scottish banking monopoly. The idea was held among Edinburgh merchants that it was the duty of a Scotsman to buy native products, and not to succumb to English tastes in clothes, furnishings or drink."[9]

The degree to which Adam Smith influenced the Glasgow

businessmen, on the other hand, is still a matter of some debate. Dugald Stewart tells us that Smith "before he quitted his situation in the university," was able "to rank some very eminent merchants among his proselytes." The Glasgow situation was certainly more favorable than that of Edinburgh. Whereas the former city looked toward Europe and the Baltic and the traditional trade, Glasgow looked towards the West and the Americas. The Act of Union had taken the parliament away from Edinburgh and created unemployment among the aristocratic servants and retainers. Glasgow, on the other hand, a city which had been loyal to the Hanoverians, was now beginning to enjoy the colonial markets, especially the American tobacco market, which had been opened up to it. The first Glasgow bank was set up in 1750 and Smith tells us in *The Wealth of Nations* that the city's trade had doubled "in about 15 years after the first erection of the banks there." Unprecedented fortunes were being made by such men as John Glassford and Andrew Cochrane who, according to Rae, were among the greatest merchants the Clyde had ever seen. It was Cochrane who founded the political economy club at Glasgow, the purpose of which was to enquire into the nature and principles of trade. According to Dr. Carlyle, Adam Smith, who became a member of this club, later acknowledged his obligations to Cochrane when he was collecting materials for *The Wealth of Nations*.

Glasgow did indeed provide Smith with an interesting "laboratory," as one writer has called it. Smith and the Glasgow businessmen no doubt provided mutual assistance in the campaign for free trade. Many businessmen, however, were free traders because it happened at the time to be expedient to be so. Smith, on the other hand, was not merely a part-time advocate; he was a free trader on principle. The businessmen supported the policy because they wanted the removal of import restrictions. But these restrictions largely affected the raw materials such as iron and linen yarn which were used in their manufactures. Such a policy, as Rae observes, did not constitute genuine support for the principle of free trade. "That was advocated as strongly from the old mercantilist strongpoint as it is now from the free-trade one; it was merely sanctioning a little addition to our imports in order to produce a much greater addition to our exports." Professor S. G. Checkland has recently made a similar point. The view that Smith practically converted Glasgow to his views is surely unlikely, he says, "in a city the prosperity of which rested upon purchasing and carrying tobacco within a monopoly situation, and selling it to a state monopoly in France."[10]

Although Smith had a personal admiration for wealthy merchants like Cochrane and Glassford it is difficult to generalize from this a liking for merchants as a class. Many of the *nouveaux riches* in the tobacco trade had new houses built for themselves which were vain and ostentatious, qualities which Smith heartily despised. According to one Glasgow biographer, many of these "tobacco barons" liked to deck themselves out in scarlet cloaks, curled wigs, cocked hats and gold-headed canes. "They were the princes of Plainstanes [the city market area], and strutted about there all day as the rulers of the destinies of Glasgow," exhibiting "a hauteur and bearing . . . assuming the air and deportment of persons immeasurably superior to all around them."[11] Moreover, not all their financial success was due to solid business virtues. Some of it stemmed from the venality of the customs officers, a situation about which Smith was peculiarly well informed.

If Smith disliked such merchants for their behavior and

taste, he must also have been more and more indisposed towards political and economic ideas that were increasingly taking hold of the minds of his professorial and aristocratic friends; for many of the landowners and lawyer intelligentsia were showing signs of becoming much more interventionist than would be compatible with Smith's views. In the 1760's, for instance, many of them favored the proposition that the grand Caledonian Canal should be constructed with the help of government subsidies. Here was "area development" (known today in Scotland as "regional development") in embryo. Smith could not disguise his opposition to such policies.

His great intellectual competitor in the bid for the minds of Glasgow men of affairs was Sir James Steuart. Returning to Glasgow just after Smith had left it in the early 1760's, Steuart set about strengthening the traditional protectionist gospel. It is true that Steuart was complaining in 1777 that Smith had persuaded what he called the "Glasgow theorists" in favor of the abolition of restrictions on corn imports; but the "theorists" to whom he was referring largely consisted of one sector, the Glasgow grain importers. Again, even they had probably cast themselves in the free-trade role because it was temporarily profitable and expedient for them to do so. (They were seeking an arrangement with Irish importers so as to monopolize Glasgow's grain supply.) Professor Checkland points out that in dealing with Scottish men of influence, Smith faced the same problem which he discussed with Edmund Burke: ". . . namely, how far must the demands of particular situations be taken into account, or how far is it proper to set out a general system of thought, as the guide to policy. Smith, in his economic thinking at least, was obliged to run counter, to a considerable degree, to the attitudes of the two principal groups of men among whom he spent the years between 1748 and 1764."[12]

The time was ripe for Smith to have a change from his home environment. By the early sixties he must have been greatly tempted at the prospect of travelling to other countries. Were not his friends all doing so? It was on the enthusiasm of friends who had come back from travels in France with stimulating accounts of its institutional life, that the Edinburgh Select Society had been founded. Smith's friend, Alan Ramsey, was in Italy; David Hume had been in Vienna and was a frequent visitor to France; even Adam Smith's own father in his lifetime had been as far afield as Burgundy. Moreover, we know from the *Edinburgh Review* (a literary magazine which Smith took a leading part in promoting in the mid-1750's) that Smith was objecting to the excessive parochialism in Scottish intellectual life. In a long letter published in the appendix to the second number of that review, Smith told the editor that he was afraid it would be impossible to "support it with any degree of spirit" as long as he persisted in confining himself almost entirely to accounts of the books published in Scotland. "The singular absurdity of some performances which you have so well represented in your first number, might divert your readers for once: but no eloquence could support a paper which consisted chiefly of accounts of such performances." Smith asked that books be selected not for their temporary "literary amusement" but for their probability of being referred to for some time to come. This would not be such a laborious task. "For though learning is cultivated in some degree in almost every part of Europe, it is in France and England only that it is cultivated with such success or reputation as to excite the attention of foreign nations." In Italy and Spain, two countries where "the first dawnings of modern genius appeared," learning had, in Smith's opinion, been extinguished. In medicine, chemistry, astronomy and mathematics, "sciences which require only plain judgement joined to labour and assiduity, without demanding a great deal of what is called either taste or genius, the Germans have been and still continue to be successful."

Among the leading countries "imagination, genius and invention, seem to be the talents of the English; taste, judgement, propriety and order, of the French." Smith's primary example of the French talents for arranging subjects in a natural and simple order was the *French Encyclopedia*, a work which he believed to promise to be "the most complete of the kind which has ever been published or attempted in any language. . . . There are above twenty Gentlemen engaged in it, all of them very eminent in their several professions, and many of them already known to foreign nations by the valuable works which they have published, particularly Mr. Alembert, Mr. Diderot, Mr. Daubenton, Mr. Rousseau of Geneva, Mr. Formey, Secretary to the Academie at Berlin, and many others."

Much as Smith admired France, England did not suffer in his relative estimation; on the contrary, as we have seen, he was proud of the inventiveness of the English, especially in natural philosophy. "The Meditations of Descartes excepted, I know nothing in French that aims at being original upon these subjects . . . but Mr. Hobbes, Mr. Locke, and Dr. Mandeville, Lord Shaftesbury, Dr. Butler, Dr. Clarke, and Mr. Hutcheson, have all of them, according to their different and inconsistent systems, endeavoured at least to be, in some measure, original." Smith, however, sensed that the initiative was slipping away from England:

This branch of the English philosophy, which seems now to be entirely neglected by the English themselves, has of late been transported into France. I observe some traces of it, not only in the Encyclopedia, but in the Theory of agreeable sentiments by Mr. De Pouilly, a work that is in many respects original; *and above all, in the late Discourse upon the origin and foundation of the inequality amongst mankind by Mr. Rousseau of Geneva.* (Italics provided)

A visitor to Adam Smith in his later life reported that Smith spoke about Rousseau "with a kind of religious respect." "Voltaire," said Smith, "set himself to correct the vices and follies of mankind by laughing at them, and sometimes by treating them with severity, but Rousseau conducts the reader to reason and truth by the attractions of sentiment and force of conviction. His 'Social Compact' will one day avenge all the persecutions he suffered."

In 1763 David Hume was moved to France as Secretary to the English Embassy in Paris. After his arrival the first letter he wrote home was to Smith. A suspected and somewhat ostracised atheist in his own country, in Paris Hume was fast becoming the idol of high society. "During the last days in particular that I have been in Fontainebleau I have *suffered* (the expression is not improper) as much flattery as almost any man has ever done in the same time, but there are few days in my life when I have been in good health that I should not rather pass over again." Before leaving Scotland, Hume had expressed the hope that he could one day meet Smith abroad. His letter from France was now no doubt calculated to encourage his economist friend still further. Smith must certainly have been pleased with a subsequent part of Hume's letter:

I had almost forgot in this effusion, shall I say, of
my misanthropy or my vanity to mention the subject
which first put my pen in my hand. D'Holbach,
whom I saw in Paris, told me that there was one
under his eye that was translating your *Theory of
Moral Sentiments*, and desired me to inform you of
it. Mr. Fitzmaurice, your old friend [a student
under Smith a few years before who had studied
law at Oxford in 1761 under Sir William Black-
stone; also the younger brother of Lord Shelburne],
interests himself strongly in this undertaking. Both
of them wish to know if you propose to make any
alteration on the work, and desire you to inform
me of your intentions in that particular.

If this letter raised the attractiveness of the prospect of a
visit to France, another one received about the same time
suddenly provided Smith with the means for such a trip. This
important letter was from Charles Townshend who, it will be
remembered, had been so impressed with Smith's *Theory of
Moral Sentiments* that he had expressed interest in the possibility of putting his stepson, the Duke of Buccleugh, under
his supervision. That was in 1759. Now in 1763 Townshend
wrote to Smith as follows:

Dear Sir: The time now drawing near when the
Duke of Buccleugh intends to go abroad, I take the
liberty of renewing the subject to you: that if you
should still have the same disposition to travel with
Him I may have the satisfaction of informing Lady
Dalkeith and His Grace of it, and of congratulating
them upon an event which I know that they, as
well as myself, have so much at heart. The Duke is
now at Eton: he will remain there until Christmas.

It is known that Smith was no admirer of absentee professors trying to hold their Scottish chairs at the same time that they held other lucrative temporary appointments. If Townshend's offer was accepted it would almost undoubtedly involve Smith's giving up his chair. Townshend apparently was well aware of this possibility; and of the consequence that the appointment of Smith as a tutor would be an expensive one. The proposition was obviously worth it however. In his letter he goes on:

> I do not enter at this moment upon the subject of establishment, because if you have no objection to the situation, I know we cannot differ about the terms. On the contrary, you will find me more solicitous than yourself to make the connections with Buccleugh satisfactory and advantageous to you as I am persuaded they will be essentially beneficial to him.

Smith accepted. The appointment included a salary of £300 a year with traveling expenses while abroad and a pension of £300 a year for life afterwards. Financially this was a very handsome offer. Smith was to render services to Buccleugh for three years. The pension thereafter was to finance the writing of *The Wealth of Nations*.

Characteristically Smith took the greatest pains to see to it that his departure from the Glasgow College in mid-session would do as little injury as possible to the University. The Faculty records on the 8th of November, 1763, reported:

> Dr. Smith represented that some interesting business would probably require his leaving the College sometime this winter, and made the following

proposals and requests to the meeting: First, that if
he should be obliged to leave the College without
finishing his usual course of lectures, he should pay
back to all his students the fees which he shall have
received from them; and that if any of them should
refuse to accept such fees, he should in that case
pay them to the University.

Second, That whatever part of the usual course of
lectures he should leave unfinished should be given
gratis to the students, by a person to be appointed
by the University, with such salary as they shall
think proper, which salary is to be paid by Dr.
Smith.

Smith's new salary from Townshend was to be double that
of his normal college annual remuneration, so he would have
been placed in a very good position to carry out the above
proposals. A successor was duly found and the fees paid back
to the students. But not without considerable difficulty. Alexander Tytler tells us in his *Life of Lord Kames:*

After concluding his last lecture, and publically
announcing from the chair that he was now taking
a final leave of his auditors, acquainting them at
the same time with the arrangements he had made,
to the best of his power, to their benefit, he drew
from his pocket the several fees of the students,
wrapped up in separate paper parcels, and beginning to call up each man by his name, he delivered
to the first who was called the money into his
hands. The young man peremptorily refused to accept it, declaring that the instruction and pleasure
he had already received was much more than he
either had repayed or ever could compensate, and a
general cry was heard from every one in the room

to the same effect. But Mr. Smith was not to be
bent from his purpose. After warmly expressing his
feelings of gratitude and the strongest sense he had
of the regard shown to him by his young friends,
he told them this was a matter betwixt him and his
own mind, and that he could not rest satisfied unless he performed what he deemed right and
proper. "You must not refuse me this satisfaction;
nay, by heavens, gentlemen, you shall not"; and
seizing by the coat the young man who stood next
him, he thrust the money into his pocket and then
pushed him from him. The rest saw it was vain to
contest the matter, and were obliged to let him
have his own way.

Smith wrote his final and formal letter of resignation from
France, in 1764. The Glasgow Senate expressed their sincere
regret ". . . at the removal of Dr. Smith, whose distinguished
proberty and amiable qualities procured him the esteem and
affection of his colleagues; whose uncommon genius, great
abilities, and extensive learning did so much honour to this
Society; his elegant and ingenious *Theory of Moral Sentiments* having recommended him to the esteem of men of
taste and literature throughout Europe."

CHAPTER X

Adam Smith in France

SMITH and his young pupil, the Duke of Buccleugh, arrived in Paris in February, 1764, where they stayed under the hospitality of David Hume. This, however, was only a temporary stopping point on their way to Toulouse, for which city they set out after only ten days in the capital. Toulouse was a provincial capital having a Parliament, a University and an Archbishopric. In addition, it was a fashionable winter residence for the nobility and the foreign visitor.

Smith and Buccleugh were received by the Vicar-General of the diocese, the Abbé Colbert, who was a cousin of David Hume and a member of the same family as the famous French minister Colbert. A month later, the Abbé wrote to Hume, "Mr. Smith is a sublime man. His heart and his mind are equally admirable. . . . The Duke, his pupil is a very amiable spirit, and does his exercises well, and is making progress in French."

It had been arranged that Smith should be introduced to the Archbishop of Toulouse; the Archbishop was rather notorious for his absence from his see and was visiting other parts of the country. Smith, whose spoken French was exceedingly bad, found to his great disappointment that his social contacts were confined mainly to one or two fellow countrymen who were visitors to the city. The first six months were indeed an anticlimax. Even his duties as tutor he found tiresome at first. In a somewhat irritable letter to Hume dated July 5th, he requested some recommendations to the Duke of Richelieu, the Marquis de Lorges, and the Intendant of the Province.

> Mr. Townshend assured me that the Duc de Choiseul was to recommend us to all the people of fashion here and everywhere else in France. We have heard nothing, however, of these recommendations, and have had our way to make as well as we could by the help of the Abbé, who is a stranger here almost as much as we. The progress indeed we have made is not very great. The Duc is acquainted with no Frenchmen whatever. I cannot cultivate the acquaintance of the few with whom I am acquainted, as I cannot bring them to our house, and I am not always at liberty to go to theirs.

But how often does genius thrive on boredom! Smith began to write a book. His letter to Hume continues: "The life I led at Glasgow was a pleasurable dissipated life in comparison of that which I lead here at present. I have begun to write a book in order to pass away the time." So was *The Wealth of Nations* born—a work which was to dominate his life for the next twelve years. However stimulating and exciting the remainder of his French sojourn was going to prove, it could not stop the course of events. The book was now to be with him wherever he went.

It is clear that soon after his arrival in France Smith began
to miss the kith and kin of Scotland. Those who wrote to him
from his home town always took care to assure him of the
health and good spirits of his mother. The latter and his
cousin, Miss Douglas, were allowed to stay on for a short
while in the house at the University which Smith had occupied. Writing to Smith in 1764, his friend Joseph Black told
him, "Mrs. Smith and Miss Douglas are perfectly well and
you made your Mother very happy with the letter which
came last night. She was particularly overjoyed at your hint
that your stay abroad was not to be so long as you expected.
She begs you will write as often as you can . . . and as to the
affair of the House, Mrs. Smith will certainly be allowed to
stay in it until Martinmass and it is even probable that she
may keep it until the Whit Sunday after."

Smith took frequent refuge in the company of a sprinkling
of fellow Scotsmen that he found in different parts of France.
On a trip to Bordeaux in August, 1764, with the Abbé Colbert, he met one of his old Scottish acquaintances, Colonel
Barré, a Frenchman who had become an English politician
and held the post of Governor of Sterling Castle. Barré, also a
friend of Hume, wrote to the latter on the 4th of September:
"I thank you for your last letter from Paris, which I received
just as Smith and his *élève* and l'Abbé Colbert were sitting
down to dine with me at Bordeaux. The latter is a very honest fellow and deserves to be a bishop; make him one if you
can. . . . Smith agrees with me in thinking that you are turned
soft by the delicacies of the French Court, and that you don't
write in that nervous manner you was remarkable for in the
more northern climates." In a letter to Hume a few weeks
later Adam Smith thanks his friend for getting them intro-
ductions to the Ambassador, Lord Hertford, and to the Duc

de Richelieu. He adds: "Our expedition to Bordeaux and another we have made since to Bagnères has made a great change upon the Duke. He begins now to familiarize himself to French company, and I flatter myself I shall spend the rest of the time we are to live together not only in Peace and contentment, but in gaity and amusement."

A little later on Smith and his party went to Montpellier to see the meeting of the States of Languedoc. These states constituted the only free local parliaments in France. In most of the remainder of the country such local governments had been suppressed. Languedoc, however, was governing its affairs so well that it was at that time being championed by many French reformers. They were particularly successful in the construction of canals, harbors and roads.

Although there is no record of any diary that Smith kept, it is certain that he was making careful note of much that he saw on these excursions. Arguing in *The Wealth of Nations* that canals are better organized by private persons than by commissioners, Smith writes:

> The canal of Languedoc cost the king of France and the province upwards of 13,000,000 of livres which amounted to upwards of £900,000 sterling. When that great work was finished, the most likely method, it was found, of keeping it in constant repair was to make a present of the tolls to Riquet the engineer, who planned and conducted the work. Those tolls constitute at present a very large estate to the different branches of the family of that gentleman, who have, therefore, a great interest to keep the work in constant repair. But had those tolls been put under the management of commissioners, who had no such interest, they might perhaps have been dissipated in ornamental and

> unnecessary expenses, while the most essential
> parts of the work were allowed to go to ruin. (II. p.
> 328)

Smith was contrasting the efficient local administration of Languedoc with that of rigid administration from the central government through the agencies of their local intendants. With such vigorous local government as that of Toulouse such things as roads, bridges, and canals were financed only in proportion to their commercial need.

> A magnificent high road cannot be made through a
> desert country where there is little or no com-
> merce, or merely because it happens to lead to the
> country villa of the intendant of the province, or to
> that of some great lord to whom the intendant
> finds it convenient to make his court. A great
> bridge cannot be thrown over a river at a place
> where nobody passes, or merely to embellish the
> view from the windows of a neighbouring palace.
> (II. p. 327)

Also in *The Wealth of Nations* Smith makes the generalization that the towns which depend mainly upon commerce for their support are usually much more prosperous and contented than large administrative centers, with large courts and retinues. From his own country he instanced Glasgow, the growing commercial center, which was much more flourishing than Edinburgh, the capital city. Similarly, his French examples included a comparison of the business city of Bordeaux, which was relatively better off than the capital city of Toulouse. Upon the cultivation of wines, Smith is also quite knowledgeable. In *The Wealth* he tells us "The vine was more affected by the differences of soils than any other fruit tree," thus illustrating the "extreme differences in the rents of the landlords." On the popular fiscal illusion that high taxes are necessary on alcoholic drinks in order to promote sobriety he is similarly illuminating:

> It deserves to be remarked too, that, if we consult experience, the cheapness of wine seems to be a cause, not of drunkenness, but of sobriety. The inhabitants of the wine countries are in general the soberest people in Europe; witness the Spaniards, the Italians, and the inhabitants of the southern provinces of France. People are seldom guilty of excess in what is their daily fare. . . . When a French regiment comes from some of the northern provinces of France, where wine is somewhat dear, to be quartered in the southern, where it is very cheap, the soldiers I have frequently heard it observed, are at first debauched by the cheapness and novelty of good wine; but after a few months residence, the greater part of them become as sober as the rest of the inhabitants. (II. pp. 70-71)

After eighteen months in Toulouse, Smith, the Duke of Buccleugh and the latter's younger brother, who had now joined the party, set out for Geneva. Their journey, according to Dugald Stewart, was by way of "a pretty extensive tour through the south of France."

The memory of Geneva that Smith was to treasure most of all was that of his conversations with the great Voltaire, then resident at Ferney, just outside the boundary of the city. It is believed that Smith visited Voltaire in his chateau by the lake five or six times. His admiration for this French genius was unbounded. The respect, however, seems to have been mutual. Smith's reputation as the author of *The Theory of*

Moral Sentiments was indeed well established in this part of the world. The son of Voltaire's intimate friend, Dr. Tronchin, a famous Geneva physician, had even been specially sent to Glasgow to attend Smith's classes. There is not much report of the conversation between the two great men. It is known, however, that apart from some convivial exchanges concerning the eccentricities of their friend, the Duc de Richelieu, the more serious conversation included the state of the constitutional upheaval that the republic of Geneva was then experiencing. Smith in his later life reported that Voltaire "expressed great aversion to the States and favoured the side of royal prerogative."

Smith and his party came to Paris from Geneva at the end of 1765. They were in time to spend a few days with David Hume, who had then just relinquished his post at the Embassy. Hume was preparing a journey to England on which he was to be accompanied by that most distinguished but wayward genius, Jean Jacques Rousseau. Although there is no evidence to prove it, it is quite probable that Smith met Rousseau in the last fortnight of 1765.

In the next few months Adam Smith was to experience the most intensive social activity of his whole life. At first he basked in the reflected glory of his close friend David Hume. Very soon, however, Smith's own personality and reputation were sufficient to sustain his popularity. Already there had been one translation into French of *The Theory of Moral Sentiments*. Rae tells us that Smith was a regular guest in almost all the famous literary salons of the time: Baron d'Holbach's, Helvétius', Madame de Geoffrin's, la Comtesse de Boufflers', Mademoiselle l'Espinasse's, and probably Madame Necker's. Smith also attended the meetings of the Physiocrats in the apartments of Dr. Quesnay. Among important fellow countrymen that Smith met at this time was Horace Walpole.

At the Baron d'Holbach's weekly dinners, Smith met Turgot and probably some of the philosophers and encyclopedists who were frequent guests there. These included Diderot, Marmontel, Raynal and Galiani. It was while dining at the table of Helvétius that Smith met Morellet, who became one of Smith's dearest friends. In his memoirs, the Abbé Morellet tells us that his conversations with Smith included "the theory of commerce, banking, public credit and various points in the great work which Smith was then meditating. . . ." Morellet, at the center of all this high intellectual activity in France, said of Smith, "I regard him still as one of the men who have made the most complete observations and analyses on all questions he treated of. . . ." Morellet himself wrote a translation of *The Wealth of Nations*.

Smith was not the only person who was busy writing an important book at this time. Another was Turgot, who was simultaneously preparing his *Formation and Distribution of Wealth*. The two men apparently were constant companions and there was obviously considerable intellectual interchange. There has been much (probably fruitless) speculation as to which author was indebted the most. It seems sensible to conclude simply that the benefits of the association were mutual. In later life Smith was to describe Turgot as "an excellent person, very honest and well-meaning, but so unacquainted with the world and human nature that it was a maxim with him, as he himself told David Hume, that whatever is right may be done."[1] This provides yet another reminder of Smith's continual and emphatic challenge to the then fashionable notion that progress was inevitable.

How fair is the observation that Smith, despite his three years in France, was not shrewd enough to foretell the impending tragedy of the French Revolution? It has now become a cliché to observe that economic distress was only one of the possible "causes" of that unhappy event. Its precise ranking with the other "causes" has always been a subject of hot debate, especially when we remember that other European countries were poorer than France. Is it fair to ask how far its relative position in the contemporary circumstances of European prosperity could have reasonably led Smith to predict political revolution in this quarter more than others?

At this time Frenchmen were certainly perplexed by the fact that the English, a poorer and much less populous nation, were making much better economic progress than they. One "explanation" which found much favor among French intellectuals was that the British social and political system was so much superior. Numerous and drastic reforms were certainly being championed by the political philosophers, most of whom were aristocrats. The animated discussion extended even to the Ministers who were actually in charge of the economy. Compared with England, France was indeed backward in administration, banking and agriculture. Moreover, an old and inefficient system of tolls on the transport of goods severely hindered internal trade. Compared with Britain, much less capital acquired in industrial cities was applied to the land. Laws of inheritance prevented the land enclosures which had been such a success in English farming. Indeed, the weight of ancient laws and customs was probably a greater hindrance than absolute monarchy or dominant nobility. As a matter of fact, the typical French noble was less well off than his counterpart in Britain; for instance, Adam Smith's protégé the Duke of Buccleugh. The usual notion of the *ancien régime*, of an aristocratic hereditary caste in this period has been exaggerated. Many of the nobles were probably the grandsons of peasants. Louis XIV, in his desperation to raise revenue had sold titles to the rich bourgeois, whose children then married into the old families. In Smith's time not more than about six per cent of the nobility were of the *ancienne noblesse*. Such variations in origins and incomes militated against any very tightly organized "power structures" among the nobility.

The French defeat in the War of Austrian Succession also hung on the French conscience at this time. The military adventures of the eighteenth-century French monarchy were certainly a serious hindrance to the economic growth. Governments were rarely solvent and had to pay higher rates of interest than British governments for borrowed money. Repudiation of some French government debt had been largely to blame.

The following quotations from *The Wealth of Nations* show not only that Smith was aware of most of the above facts, but also that while he was quite critical of French economic conditions, his judgement was always a balanced or relative one.

> The corn-lands of England, . . . are better cultivated that those of France, and the corn-lands of France are said to be much better cultivated than those of Poland. (I. p. 5)
> The silks of France are better and cheaper than those of England, because the silk manufacture, at least under the present high duties upon the importation of raw silk, does not so well suit the climate of England as that of France. But the hard-ware and the coarse woollen of England are beyond all comparison superior to those of France, are much cheaper too in the same degree of goodness. (I. p. 5)

France is perhaps in the present times not so rich a country as England; and though the legal rate of interest has in France frequently been lower than in England, the market rate has generally been higher; for there, as in other countries, they have several very safe and easy methods of evading the law. (I. p. 101)

The wages of labour are lower in France than in England. When you go from Scotland to England, the difference which you may remark between the dress and countenance of the common people in the one country and in the other, sufficiently indicates the difference in their condition. The contrast is still greater when you return from France. France, though no doubt a richer country than Scotland, seems not to be going forwards so fast. It is a common and even popular opinion in the country, that it is going backwards; an opinion which, I apprehend, is ill-founded even with regard to France, but which nobody can possibly entertain with regard to Scotland, who sees the country now; and who saw it twenty or thirty years ago. (I. p. 101)

Smith found particularly long apprenticeship schemes in France. We know his views on these: "Long apprenticeships are altogether unnecessary. . . . The institution of long apprenticeships has no tendency to pull young people to industry. The institution of long apprenticeships can give no security that insufficient workmanship shall not frequently be exposed to public sale." (I. p. 137) In Scotland, three years was the common term of apprenticeship. There was no other country in Europe in which corporation laws were so little oppressive. In Paris, in contrast, ". . . five years is the term required in a great number; but before any person can be qualified to exercise the trade as a master, he must in many of them, serve five years more as a journeyman."

On more detailed matters:

> In France, and even in Scotland, where labour is somewhat better rewarded than in France, the labouring poor seldom eat butcher's-meat, except upon holidays, and other extraordinary occasions. (I. p. 211)

> When the king's troops, when his household or his officers of any kind pass though any part of the country, the yeomanry were bound to provide them with horses, carriages, and provisions, at a price regulated by the purveyor. Great Britain is, I believe, the only monarchy in Europe where the oppression of purveyance has been entirely abolished. It still subsists in France and Germany. (I. p. 417)

> The ancient lords, though extremely unwilling to grant themselves any pecuniary aids to their sovereign, easily allowed him to tallage, as they call it, their tenants, and had not knowledge enough to foresee how much this must in the end affect their own revenue. The taille, as it still subsists in France, may serve as an example of those ancient tallages. It is a tax upon the supposed profits of the farmer, which they estimate by the stock which he has upon the farm. . . . Should any stock happen to accumulate in the hands of a French farmer, the taille is almost equal to a prohibition of its ever being employed upon the land. (I. p. 417)

Finally, and inevitably, Smith attacks the incubus of Mercantilism:

> The French have been particularly forward to favour their own manufactures by restraining the importation of such foreign goods as could come into competition with them. In this consisted a

great part of the policy of Mr. Colbert, who, notwithstanding his great abilities, seems in this case
to have been imposed upon by the sophistry of
merchants and manufacturers, who are always
demanding a monopoly against their countrymen.
It is at present the opinion of the most intelligent
men in France that his operations of this kind have
not been beneficial to his country. (II. p. 42)

This was indeed an impressive list of failures and weak-
nesses, but was it an adequate basis on which to predict revolution? Smith's purpose in writing *The Wealth of Nations*
was to criticize institutions rather than particular countries.
His strongest attacks were made upon the apparently immov-
able solid blocks of ancient laws and customs and absurd
mercantilist economic policies, both of which were severely
stifling trade and prosperity. In his survey, France certainly
received poor marks relative to other countries; but few
other countries receive high marks either. Conditions of economic frustration, while they may provide a necessary condition, do not provide a sufficient condition for political revolution. Even if Smith had wanted to, it would have been an
extremely difficult task to forecast such an event, or at least, its
precise timing. The Revolution, after all, did not occur until
twenty years after his visit. By that time the scene had
changed in several details. Moreover, when it did come, the
French Revolution, like the Industrial Revolution, was unprecedented in scale. It is only too easy for twentieth-century
observers, with their benefit of hindsight, to make excessive
demands for clairvoyance from the writers of the 1760's and
1770's.

Did Adam Smith's French tour significantly benefit the
quality of his writings as an economist? In his biography,

Dugald Stewart thought it a waste of time. Had Smith not gone to France and interrupted that "studious leisure for which nature seems to have destined him" he might have been able to "accomplish those literary projects which had flattered the ambition of his youthful genius." Professor George Stigler, commenting recently on an account of the foreign tour in 1797 of another political economist, T. R. Malthus, concludes, playfully perhaps, ". . . no important economic idea of which I have ever heard had an empirical debt to foreign (or domestic) travel. If Fulbright wished to encourage purely scientific work, he should have given grants to live for nine months near a good American library . . ."[2] While science may owe little to travel, however, such travels do expose a scholar to the world in a way which his studies never can. And the biographer has a legitimate interest in the host of smaller details in a man's life that are apt to be revealed in sharper focus in foreign company. We seek to bring to light his foibles, aversions and amusements. We want to know what kind of companion, how reliable a friend, how amusing a conversationalist?

We know that Smith was always less forthcoming in a group than in the company of one. In Paris this was particularly so. Dupont de Nemours told J. B. Say that the *économistes* (physiocrats) at their meetings in the apartments of the king's physician, Dr. Quesnay, in the Palace of Versailles, looked upon Smith as "a judicious and simple man, and apparently nothing more." This was partly, however, because, as the same observer explains, Smith had not by then shown to the world the stuff he was made of on the subject of economics. Dupont compares extracts from Smith's subsequent writing with Smith's opinions on the same subjects as expressed in private. On one particular item he once said,

"Smith in his own room, or in that of a friend, as I have seen him when we were fellow-disciples of M. Quesnay, would not have said that."[3]

Of the loyalty and integrity which Smith showed to his friends there can be no doubt. One small piece of evidence on this comes to us at this time in the form of a letter addressed to his friend David Hume. It will be remembered that Hume had gone to England as host to his friend Rousseau. By the middle of 1766 the French guest was living in a comfortable establishment in Derbyshire on a pension supplied by Hume. Since Rousseau was known to be a man with a deep persecution complex, his friends predicted that his relationship with Hume could not last very long. They were right. Rousseau eventually wrote to Hume declaring "that his horrible designs were at last found out."

Normally the most patient of men, Hume this time lost his temper. Preparing to expose the whole quarrel in writing to public judgement, he wrote to Smith asking him to explain the situation to their common friends in Paris. Smith wrote back promptly:

> Paris, 6th July, 1766. My Dear Friend—I am thoroughly convinced that Rousseau is as great a rascal as you and as every man here believe him to be. Yet let me beg of you not to think of publising anything to the world upon the very great impertinence which he has been guilty of . . . stand this ridicule; expose his brutal letter, but without giving it out of your own hand, so that it may never be printed, and, if you can, laugh at yourself, and I will pawn my life that before three weeks are at an end this little affair which at present gives you so much uneasiness shall be understood to do you as much honour as anything that has ever happened

to you. By endeavouring to unmask before the public this hypocritical pedant, you run the risk of disturbing the tranquility of your whole life. By leaving him alone he cannot give you a fortnight's uneasiness. . . . Your whole friends here wish you not to write, the Baron, d'Almbert, Madame Riccoboni, Mademoiselle Rianecourt, M. Turgot, etc. etc. M. Turgot, a friend every way worthy of you, desired me to recommend this advice to you in a particular manner as his most earnest entreaty and opinion. He and I are both afraid you are surrounded with evil councillors, and that the advice of your English *literati*, who are themselves accustomed to publishing all their little gossiping stories in newspapers, may have too much influence upon you. Remember me to Mr. Walpole, and believe me, etc.

Smith's strong aversion to "gossiping stories in newspapers" is characteristic. It partly explains his own reluctance to write letters and his anxiety to keep his personal life as much of a closed book as possible; characteristics which, while no doubt prudent in themselves, can only be a source of regret to the biographer.

The Rousseau episode reminds us of another instance of Smith's anxiety to protect his friends from gossip-mongers, this time in his later years. In 1780 a young interviewer from Glasgow mentioned to him some story about Burke seducing a young lady. Smith promptly declared it an invention. "I imagine that you have got that fine story out of some of the Magazines. If anything can be lower than the Reviews, they are so. . . . As to Mr. Burke, he is a worthy, honest man, who married an accomplished girl without a shilling of fortune."[4]

Gossip is one thing, sincere biography is another. Smith

himself could not have objected to his own biographer sifting the smallest details of his life, provided he did so from the best motives. After all, it was Smith who taught the celebrated Boswell how to write! And Boswell was especially delighted with his professor's observation that we are glad to know the minutest detail about a great man, as, for example, that Milton wore latchets instead of buckles in his shoes.[5]

Smith had now been made fully aware of the much more prominent role that women in France played in political and intellectual life. "Intellectual" dinner parties and literary discussions were here typically sponsored by the feminine sex. Moreover, the lady organizers did not confine themselves merely to the role of hostess; they were eloquent participants in the discussions. Rae tells us, for instance, that the Duchesse d'Enville, whom Smith had visited often in Geneva, was a woman of great ability and was the alleged inspirer of all Turgot's political and social ideas.

How did Smith fare in this sudden change of environment? Did he easily make the change from the all-male Glasgow club to the charm and chatter of the Parisian soirée? We know that after once being drawn into a conversation by the request for his opinion on some matter, Smith would often become so carried away in the pursuit of some idea as eventually to become much less aware of those around him. Could it be that the lady hostesses were unusually good audiences? Would Smith sometimes "awake" suddenly from his absent-mindedness and sense that his listeners were "too good"? Once he suspected that his "impartial spectators" were perhaps not so impartial, we can easily imagine him resorting to hasty retreats and embarrassed silences.

It is known from letters to Smith's friends that once he was back in Britain there were several enquiries after him by

French ladies. Ten years after his visit, his friend Adam Ferguson wrote to Smith to say that the Duchesse d'Enville asked frequently after him. Ferguson added that although the Duchesse had complained about Smith's spoken French she had nevertheless learned his (Smith's) language before he had left Paris in 1766.

In March, 1766, David Hume wrote to the Comtesse de Bouffler-Rouvel:

> I am glad you have taken my friend Smith under your protection. You will find him a man of true merit, though perhaps his sedentary life may have hurt his air and appearance as a man of the world.

The Comtesse replied a few weeks later:

> I think I told you that I have made the acquaintance of Mr. Smith, and that for the love of you I had given him a very hearty welcome. I am now reading his *Theory of Moral Sentiments*. I am not very far advanced with it yet, but I believe it will please me.

All this for the love of Hume? According to Rae, in 1770, when the two sons of Smith's friend, Sir Gilbert Elliot, visited her, ". . . they found her at her studies in her bedroom, and talking of translating the book, if she had time, because it contained such just ideas about sympathy. She added that the book had come into great vogue in France, and that Smith's doctrine of sympathy bade fair to supplant David Hume's immaterialism as the fashionable opinion, especially with the ladies." (Rae adds, incidentally, that the best translation into French of *The Theory of Moral Sentiments* was eventually published by another lady, the widow of Condorcet.)

Another frequent resort of Smith was the salon of Mademoiselle de l'Espinasse, which, Rae tells us, differed from the others by the greater variety of the guests; ". . . to her unpretending apartments ambassadors, princesses, marshals of France, and financiers came, and met with men of letters like Grimm, Condillac, and Gibbon."

Amidst various other occupations in Paris, Stewart tells us that Smith took every opportunity to cultivate his taste for the fine arts. Having already read widely the writings of the French dramatists, he now made several visits to the French theatre to see their works enacted. Smith was a frequent guest of Madame Riccoboni, who was one of the most celebrated novelists in France, having previously had a stage career. In the 1790 edition of his *Theory of Moral Sentiments* Smith ranks her with Voltaire and Racine, as instructors in "the refinements and delicacies of love and friendship." There is a letter from her to David Garrick, the English actor, which contains the remarkable outburst:

> Oh ces écossais! ces chiens d'écossais! Ils viennent me plaire et m'affliger. Je suis comme ces folles jeunes filles qui écoutent un amant sans penser au regret, toujours voisin du plaisir. Grondez-moi, battez-moi, tuez-moi! Mais j'aime Mr. Smith, je l'aime beaucoup.

This letter was to be delivered by Smith on his arrival home. Madame Riccoboni wrote to Garrick a few months later asking whether the "charming" Mr. Smith had in fact delivered it.

Vous ne l'avez pas encore vu, Mr. Smith? c'est la
plus distraite créature! mais c'est une des plus
aimables. Je l'aime beaucoup et je l'estime encore
d'avantage.

We could also tell of yet another lady who made a brief
encounter with Smith during his French tour, this time a
marquise of talent and wit who was staying in the same hotel
as Smith, on one of his excursions to Abbeville; of how she
was so overcome by Smith's personal charms that she fell in
love with him; how after many persistent efforts she eventually had to abandon her attempt at conquest; and how Smith
could neither endure her nor conceal his embarrassment. But
we shall end our speculations with a reference from Smith's
personal acquaintance and biographer, Dugald Stewart. According to him, Smith had an early attachment with a lady
who remained single and at 80 years of age still carried traces
of her former beauty. After this early disappointment, Stewart tells us, Smith laid aside all thoughts of marriage. Smith
clearly covered up his tracks very well on this subject. But he
could not complain of posterity's inquisitiveness, or of those
who concluded from available evidence that Smith must have
been like the Oxford don who once confided: "There are two
things I know of only from books, one is war and the other is
love."

Whatever his adventures in Paris, there was one event in
August, 1766, which seriously reminded Smith of his responsibilities as a tutor. The Duke of Buccleugh had been to
Compiègne on a hunting party with the King and the Court.
After a hearty supper with "a vast quantity of salad and some
cold punch" the Duke was struck with sickness and fever. In
a solicitous letter to the Duke's stepfather, Charles Townshend, Adam Smith wrote:

> I sent for Quenay [Quesnay the economist] first
> ordinary physician to the king. He sent me word
> he was ill. . . . The Duke was in the same profuse
> sweat which he had been in all day and all the
> preceding night. In this situation Quenay declared
> that it was improper to do anything until the sweat
> should be over. He only ordered some cooling
> ptisane drink. Quenay's illness made it impossible
> for him to return next day (Monday), and de la
> Saone (first physician to the Queen) has waited on
> the Duke ever since, to my entire satisfaction.

Smith told Townshend to expect a letter from him by every
post until the Duke had perfectly recovered. ". . . I never stir
from his room from eight in the morning till ten at night,
and watch for the smallest change that happens to him."

By the autumn of 1766 homesickness began to predominate. "Though I am very happy here", he wrote to Millar the
London bookseller, "I long passionately to rejoin my old
friends, and if I had once got fairly to your side of the water,
I think I should never cross it again." He returned to London with the Duke of Buccleugh in October, 1766. In a letter
to Dugald Stewart many years later, the Duke wrote that he
had been with Smith for nearly three years: ". . . without the
slightest disagreement or coolness, and, on my part, with
every advantage that could be expected from the society of
such a man."

Had Smith really been the ideal tutor? Not everybody at
this time thought so. In his autobiography Dr. Carlyle said of
him: "He was the most absent man in company I ever knew,"
and "he appeared very unfit for the intercourse of the world
as a travelling tutor." Carlyle even suggested that the Duke's
stepfather, Charles Townshend, arranged the tour "for his
own glory of having sent an eminent Scotch philosopher to

travel with the Duke." The account of Smith's tour in France now ends; but with an episode of tragedy the suddenness of which caused shock and surprise to all. The younger of Smith's two pupils, the Honourable Hew Campbell Scott, was assassinated in the streets of Paris, on the 18th of October, 1766. There is no record of Smith's opinion of this unfortunate young man, who had only attained the age of nineteen at the time of his death. Smith and the Duke of Buccleugh, accompanied by Lord George Lennox, Hume's successor as secretary of legation, traveled immediately to London, bringing the remains of their unfortunate companion with them.

Smith was never to travel abroad again. Neither was he again to undertake the responsibilities of a personal tutorship. As for his opinion on the value of foreign travel as an educational influence upon the young, it was to be contained in a paragraph in *The Wealth of Nations* ten years later:

> In England, it becomes every day more and more the custom to send young people to travel in foreign countries immediately upon their leaving school, and without sending them to any university. Our young people, it is said, generally return home much improved by their travels. A young man who goes abroad at 17 or 18, and returns home at one and twenty, returns three or four years older than he was when he went abroad; and at that age it is very difficult not to improve a good deal in three or four years. In the course of his travels, he generally acquires some knowledge of one or two foreign languages; knowledge, however, which is seldom sufficient to enable him either to speak or write them with propriety. In other respects, he commonly returns home more conceited, more

unprincipled, more dissipated, and more incapable of any serious application either to study or to business, than he could well have become in so short a time, had he lived at home. By travelling so very young, by spending in the most frivolous dissipation the most precious years of his life, at a distance from the inspection and control of his parents and relations, every useful habit, which the earlier parts of his education might have had some tendency to form in him, instead of being rivetted and confirmed, is almost necessarily either weakened or effaced. . . . By sending his son abroad, a father delivers himself, at least for some time from so disagreeable an object as that of a son unemployed, neglected, and going to ruin before his eyes. (II. p. 378)

CHAPTER XI

The Kirkcaldy Retreat

ANXIOUS as Smith was to return to Scotland and to the writing of his book, he was obliged to stay on for a few months in London. One reason was that he was publishing with Millar, the London bookseller, a new edition of his *Theory of Moral Sentiments*. The second reason is connected with the fact that in the year of Smith's return, the disturbing question of the American Colonies had begun to flare up. The colonists were infuriated with the Stamp Act which had been passed in the previous year. Many of them were now refusing to pay for English goods stocked in their shops and warehouses. Although the Rockingham Whigs eventually succeeded in getting the Stamp Act repealed, Townshend [Buccleugh's stepfather], the new Chancellor—being particularly pressed for revenue now, in 1767—imposed upon the Colonies the famous Tea Duties. One of Smith's jobs in London, according to one writer, was ". . . to devil for Townshend, answer questions of fact, suggest ideas on general principles, and furnish the latest information on French finance."[1] Meanwhile, the statesman Shelburne engaged Smith for research into legal and historical aspects of colonial policy. It is difficult, however, to believe that Smith, who really was a supporter of Rockingham, had his heart in these jobs. Smith nowhere tells us his opinion of Townshend, but it is not likely that he was unduly taken with the man who was subsequently known as "the Chancellor whose irresponsibilities led to the loss of the American Colonies."

On the 3rd of May, 1767, the Duke of Buccleugh was married. This event was probably another cause for Smith's tarrying in London. In the meantime it seems he was doing the usual social rounds (he had been to London for the first time in 1761, prior to his French tour, and was thus already acquainted with some of the London clubs). According to one anecdote of this period we must conclude that Smith's French tour had not cured him of absent-mindedness. A Mr. Damer, who paid Smith a visit in his London apartment one morning, found the Scotsman sitting down to breakfast. Becoming, as usual, absorbed in the discussion, Smith took a piece of bread and butter, and after rolling it round and round put it into the teapot. After a few more sentences of conversation he poured the water on it. Eventually he poured himself a cup and on tasting it declared it to be the worst cup of tea he had ever met with.

In the summer of 1767 he at last returned to Scotland and took up residence in a house in Kirkcaldy with his mother and cousin. It was a substantial building with 20 windows facing into the High Street, and a rear garden 50 feet wide running down to the beach. The house was pulled down in 1844, but there remain the high wall and the narrow public footpath on the other side of it which were there in Smith's time. The pathway, which is flanked on the other side by another high wall, now bears the name "Adam Smith's Close."

It was in this environment, with his relatives and lifelong friends, that Smith settled down in earnest to writing his masterpiece. He wrote to Hume from Kirkcaldy on June 9th, 1767:

> My business here is study, in which I have been very deeply engaged for about a month past. My amusements are long solitary walks by the sea side. You may judge how I spend my time. I feel myself, however, extremely happy, comfortable, and contented. I never was perhaps more so in all my life.

Smith's friends were going to find him difficult to shift from this happy position for several years to come. Only occasionally would he even to go see friends in Edinburgh. There was, however, one minor social obligation that he was yet to fulfill. At the end of the summer he spent a few weeks at Dalkeith House, where the Duke of Buccleugh and his wife were taking up residence. On September 15th he wrote to Hume:

> They begin to open their house on Monday next, and I flatter myself, will both be very agreeable to the people of this country. I am not sure that I have ever seen a more agreeable woman than the Duchess. I am sorry that you are not here, because I am sure that you would be perfectly in love with her. I shall probably be here some weeks. . . . I should be glad to know the true history of Rousseau before and since he left England. You may perfectly depend upon my never quoting you to any living soul upon that subject.

It had been planned that on that day, September 15th, the

Duke of Buccleugh was to entertain his neighbors around his estate and that Smith was to be there to help receive them. However, this event had to be postponed because of the sudden death of the Duke's father, Townshend. The plan was fulfilled about three weeks later and about 50 ladies and gentlemen of the neighborhood attended. Dr. Carlyle, who was present, tells us (in his autobiography) that the fare was sumptuous but the company was formal and dull. The latter he attributed to the fact that the guests were all strangers to their host and hostess. As for Adam Smith, he was, according to Carlyle, "ill qualified to promote the jollity of a birthday." Possibly thinking that he himself was a better candidate for the job, Carlyle added that the social debut of the young Duke and his wife would have been more efficient "if they had brought down a man of more address than he [Smith] was."

Dalkeith House, then known as Dalkeith Palace, still stands today, a proud example of an eighteenth-century mansion. It now houses the registered offices of the present Duke of Buccleugh's Estate and contains many historical treasures. These, according to a recent visitor, include the sword of General Townshend, who took over from Wolfe at Quebec, the white silk shirt worn by Monmouth at his execution, and the records of the Estate and its family stretching over centuries—"records of medieval travel, boxes of seals, estate maps, and estate accounts, and letters to and from the successive occupants of the house."[2]

Smith was always an honored guest at Dalkeith Palace for the rest of his life. Many other distinguished visitors were entertained there. One of these, Lord Brougham, gives us another anecdote of our author's absence of mind. At dinner Adam Smith once apparently broke out into a strong condemnation of the public conduct of some leading statesman of the day. Suddenly perceiving that statesman's nearest relative on the opposite side of the table, he stopped short, but then went on to mutter to himself, "Deil care, deil care, it's all true."

For several years after this there is nothing of much consequence in his life except the writing of the book. Two years after Smith's return to Scotland, David Hume, having lost his place with a change of ministry, returned to Edinburgh. He wrote in August, 1769:

> Dear Smith: I am glad to have come within sight of you, and to have a view of Kirkcaldy from my windows, but as I wish also to be within speaking terms of you, I wish we could concert measures for that purpose. . . . I am also tired of travelling as much as you ought naturally to be of staying at home. I therefore propose to you to come hither and pass some days with me in this solitude. I want to know what you have been doing, and purpose to exact a rigorous account of the methods in which you have employed yourself during your retreat. I am positive you are in the wrong in many of your speculations, especially when you have the misfortune to differ from me.

A few months later, Hume teasingly writes: "How can you so much as entertain a thought of publishing a book full of reason, sense, and learning to those wicked abandoned madmen?" By now Smith had probably completed his first draft. For six years more, however, he was to be constantly changing, augmenting and polishing the new work.

In January, 1772, Hume continues to press Smith for a visit: "I shall not take any excuse from your own state of health, which I suppose only a subterfuge invented by indolence and love of solitude. Indeed, my dear Smith, if you continue to harken to complaints of this nature, you will cut yourself out entirely from human society, to the great loss of both parties." Smith and Hume were at this time reading, in the original, Italian historians and poets; this letter shows them exchanging views on such writings.

In September, 1772, Smith wrote to his friend Pulteney. This letter shows further evidence of how Smith's ill health was interrupting his work. "My book would have been ready for the press by the beginning of this winter, but interruptions occasioned partly by bad health, arising from want of amusement and thinking too much upon one thing, and partly by the avocations above mentioned, would oblige me to retard its publication for a few months longer."

There is reference to the East India Company which, at that time, was under severe attack. Pulteney had apparently recommended that the Directors put Smith forward as a member of the proposed Commission into their administration and accounts. This Commission in fact was not appointed and no significant reforms were made. Smith obviously spent many weeks of hard work upon this subject; the fruits of his work are evident in *The Wealth of Nations*, where the Company receives some of his most devastating indictments.

In November, 1772, David Hume was urging his friend to publish the book quickly, to break off his studies and to have some relaxation:

Dear Smith: I should agree with your Reasoning if I could trust your Resolution. Come hither for some weeks about Christmas; dissipate yourself a little; return to Kirkcaldy; finish your work before autumn; go to London, print it, return and settle in this town, which suits your studious, independent turn, even better than London. Execute this plan faithfully, and I forgive you.

But Smith was still reflecting, writing, polishing, correcting and no doubt pacing the beach at Kirkcaldy. What was his mode of working? What was his daily routine? Dugald Stewart tells us that he dictated his work to a secretary. Moreover, he composed his sentences standing. A visitor to his study in the 1820's had his attention drawn to a mark on the wall which, he was assured, was caused by Smith's rubbing his wig sideways against the wall as he dictated. Characteristically, the biographer Rae seizes upon this detail with the scrupulous observation: "His head being dressed, in the ordinary style of that period, with pomatum, could not fail to make a mark on the wall."

There is a legendary story of this period to the effect that one Sunday morning, lost in thought as usual, Smith walked into his garden in an old dressing gown. Instead of going into the house, he drifted onto the turnpike road. Eventually he walked as far as the town of Dunfermline, several miles from his home, and only came to his wits when disturbed by the noise of people going to church.

The book was obviously making heavy demands on him. He was now in the ninth year of writing; but every day the relentless work would continue; walking, standing, dictating, correcting. Would the work never be finished?

CHAPTER XII

London: The Eve of Publication

BY the Spring of 1773 the exhaustive work had told alarmingly on Smith's health and spirits. Indeed, it seems that he was afraid he might die before the book got through the press. Starting out for London with the manuscript, he broke his journey at Edinburgh to write a formal letter to Hume, appointing him his executor: "As I have left the care of all my literary papers to you, I must tell you that except those which I carry along with me, there are none worth the publishing but a fragment of a great work which contains a history of the astronomical systems that were successively in fashion down to the time of Descartes. . . . Unless I die very suddenly, I shall take care that the Papers I carry with me shall be carefully sent to you." Smith was in London by May, 1773. Fortunately his health soon recovered. He was to spend over two more years completing the book.

The American question was then the chief topic of the day in all the London clubs and coffee houses, and Smith directed more and more of his writing to the subject. Other topical matters were also being assimilated in Smith's work. For instance, in the year he arrived in London there was marshaled

through the House of Commons a bill which modified the
bounties on the export of grain. In the first edition of *The
Wealth of Nations* Smith criticised this legislation for not
getting rid of the bounties altogether and indeed, for being
inferior to that which preceded it.

He was now taking more time off from writing, a fact
which no doubt partly explained the improvement in his
health. Smith was an active clubman, enjoyed a reasonable
social life and moved freely in intellectual society. In May of
1773 he was admitted to the Royal Society. Later we have a
report of him at dinner at Sir Joshua Reynolds' along with
Johnson, Burke, Gibbon and others. With Gibbon, Smith attended Dr. William Hunter's famous lectures on anatomy.
Hunter, incidentally, was a private teacher who had set himself up outside the jurisdiction of the University Medical
Monopoly, which regarded as a quack anyone outside their
system.

Smith's views on this subject are preserved for us in a letter
he wrote from London the next year to his friend, Dr. W.
Cullen, of the University of Edinburgh. Cullen, on behalf of
his colleagues, had presented a memorial to the Duke of Buccleugh asking him to sponsor legislation in Parliament so
that, in effect, a monopoly could be set up in Scotland similar
to that in London. Wisely, the Duke of Buccleugh referred
Cullen to his old tutor, Adam Smith. Smith's reply is particularly interesting because it illustrates not only the vigor of his
thought, but the pungency, style and wit of the man who had
now reached the apex of his literary form. Telling Cullen
first that his proposal would strengthen still further the existing monopoly power of (endowed) universities which were
to grant the examination certificates, he continued: "Monopo-
lists seldom make good work, and a lecture which a certain

number of students must attend, whether they profit by it or no is certainly not very likely to be a good one." But a free market in the realm of medicine? Many twentieth-century readers may protest that this is extremism in defence of doctrine. Granted that the average man is responsible enough to choose his own butcher, it does not follow, so they will argue, that he can be trusted to choose his own doctor. Smith's sprightly answer will at least give them food for thought:

> That Doctors are sometimes fools as well as other people, is not, in the present times, one of those profound secrets which is known only to the learned. The title is not so very imposing, and it very seldom happens to a man that he trusts his health to another merely because the other is a doctor. The person so trusted has almost always either some knowledge or some craft which would procure him nearly the same trust, though he was not decorated with any such title.

Because a person had a university degree which licensed him to practice as a doctor, did this obviate people's problem of choice? Smith pointed out that the holders of degrees still varied in their ability. Some doctors had taken twice as long as others to graduate, for instance. In some cases, especially at poor universities, the examination was perfunctory and the degree obtained mainly by "doing time" and paying fees at the university. Furthermore, by giving an aura of worthiness to a person of low competence, the degree title might also have extended his practice "and consequently his field for doing mischief; it is not improbable too, that it may increase his presumption and consequently his disposition to do mischief." Moreover, Smith argued that the degree-licensing system would so strengthen a growing monopoly as to lead to still higher prices. Many of the public would then be deprived of medical attention altogether for want of money. "Had the universities of Oxford and Cambridge been able to maintain themselves in the exclusive privilege of graduating all the doctors who could practise in England, the price of feeling a pulse might by this time have risen from two and three guineas, the price which it has now happily arrived at, to double or triple that sum; and English physicians might, and probably would, have been at the same time the most ignorant and quackish in the world."

Smith chided the doctors for affecting to champion society's interests when all the time their real purpose was to prevent the erosion of their own incomes:

> Stage doctors, I must observe, do not much excite the indignation of the faculty; more reputable quacks do. The former are too contemptible to be considered as rivals: they only poison the poor people and the copper pence which are thrown up to them in handkerchieves could never find their way to the pockets of their regular physician. It is otherwise with the latter: they sometimes intercept a part of what perhaps would have been better bestowed in another place. Do not all the old women in the country practise physic without inciting murmour or complaint? And if here and there a graduated doctor should be as ignorant as an old woman where can be the great harm? The beardless old woman takes no fees; the bearded one does, and it is this circumstance, I strongly suspect, which exasperates his brethren so much against him.

Dr. William Hunter, whose lectures Smith and Gibbon were at this time attending, was a distinguished pioneer in the field of anatomy but did not have a university education. Cullen's proposal included the condition that no person should be admitted to the examination for degrees unless he brought a certificate that he had studied at least two years in some university. Smith asks him:

> Would not such a regulation be oppressive upon all private teachers, such as the Hunters, Hudson, Fordyce, etc. The scholars of such teachers surely merit whatever honour or advantage a degree can confer much more than the greater part of those who have spent many years in some universities, where the different branches of medical knowledge are either not taught at all, or are taught so superficially that they had as well not been taught at all. When a man has learnt his lesson very well, it surely can be of little importance where or from whom he has learnt it.

All this was further grist to Smith's mill. Such material was to reappear in *The Wealth of Nations* in forms like the following:

"The privileges of graduates in arts, in law, *physic* and divinity, when they can be obtained only by residing a certain number of years in certain universities, necessarily force a certain number of students to such universities, independent of the merit or reputation of the teachers." (Italics provided) (II. p. 368) Smith's reasoning was presumably triumphant at the time, for Cullen's scheme was not successful.[1]

Letters to Smith in London were addressed to The British Coffee House on Cockspur Street. At this time a weekly dining club was held there, and it included among its many distinguished members Goldsmith, Sir Joshua Reynolds, Garrick and the famous architect Robert Adam. In 1775 Smith was admitted to the celebrated Literary Club run by Dr. Johnson, Edmund Burke and Joshua Reynolds. Reynolds and Gibbon were present on the night of his election. Smith's conversation in this company is reported to have had a "decisive professorial manner." One club member subsequently told a friend, "I have often told him after half an hour's conversation, 'Sir, you have said enough to make a book'." Boswell describes Smith's conversation as showing "a mind crowded with all manner of subjects." His voice was apparently rather harsh and stammering, and especially among strangers he often appeared embarrassed. One of his contemporaries speaks of Smith's "captivating" smile of approbation, another states that "in the society of those he loved his features were often brightened with a smile of inexpressible benignity."

By the mid-1770's the American question was really overshadowing all other topics and Smith pursued with still greater vigor his study of the whole problem of colonial administration. He may have had the opportunity of discussing the matter with another friend, Benjamin Franklin, who was in London at the time. He considered the separation of America from the mother country as a possible solution to the problem but he was not convinced, as was Hume, that such an event was inevitable. He was interested in a policy of closer union. He wanted the colonies to pay their share of taxes and, in return, to enjoy legitimate constitutional privileges. He thought it was particularly wrong to place restrictions on the commerce of the colonies where the commerce of Great Britain was free. Taxation *with* representation, that was the true solution. The Duke of Buccleugh informed

Hume at this time that Adam Smith was "very zealous" in American affairs. He was much more concerned about the event, it seems, than was Hume. Both of them however condemned the war and the prevailing colonial policy.

But what of Smith's magnum opus? Was it never to appear? His friends were getting impatient. Hume wrote to Smith in February, 1776: "By all accounts your book has been printed long ago, yet it has never been so much as advertised. What is the reason? If you wait till the fate of Bavaria be decided, you may wait long." However, within only a few days of this letter the book was out. The book was out! *An Inquiry Into the Nature and Causes of The Wealth of Nations* by Adam Smith, LL.D. and F.R.S., formerly Professor of Moral Philosophy in the University of Glasgow, was published on March 9th, 1776. When, four months later, the American states were declaring their independence, first-edition copies of Smith's book were still being sold. Thus the work which had devoured so many years of peace was now born in war.

CHAPTER XIII

The Wealth of Nations

ON the 1st of April, 1776, Gibbon wrote from London to Adam Ferguson: "What an excellent work is that with which our common friend Mr. Adam Smith has enriched the public! An extensive science in a single book, and the most profound ideas expressed in the most perspicuous language." On the same day David Hume wrote: "EUGE! BELLE! DEAR MR. SMITH—I am much pleased with your performance, and the perusal of it has taken me from a state of great anxiety. It was a work of so much expectation, by yourself, by your friends, and by the public, that I trembled for its appearance, but I am now much relieved." Also, in the same month Hugh Blair (Minister of the High Church, Edinburgh) wrote to Smith:

> My Dear Sir: I cannot forebear writing to congratulate you upon your book. I have just finished it; and though from what you read to me some years ago, and from the great attention which I knew you had bestowed upon the subject I expected much, but I confess you have exceeded my expectation. . . . I do think the age is highly indebted to

you, and I wish they may be duly sensible of the obligation. . . . Your work ought to be, and I am persuaded will in some degree become, the commercial Code of Nations. I did not read one chapter of it without acquiring much light and instruction. I am convinced that since Montesquieu's *Esprit des Lois*, Europe has not received any publication which tends so much to enlarge and rectify the ideas of mankind.

Such was the reception of friends to the work which had taken its author twelve years to write and perhaps as long again in previous preparation. Its impact upon the world was not quite so immediate, but its influence rose like a gradually and inexorably swelling tide. The first edition was completely sold out in six months, surprising the publishers beyond all expectation. Several years were to elapse before the book was actually alluded to in Parliament. There were, however, clear signs of immediate influence upon parliamentary legislation. Lord North's budget of the following year (1777) introduced two new "Smithian" taxes, one on manservants and the other on property sold by auction. Both these taxes were advocated in *The Wealth of Nations*. Similarly, the budget of 1778 introduced the inhabited-house duty and the malt tax. By 1779 statesmen were seeking the advice of Smith on matters of current importance such as the Irish economic problem.

What kind of book was it after all? How was it received in its own time and what has been the judgement of posterity? In retrospect some will see the work largely as a brilliant period piece. It was indeed rich with illustrations from the eighteenth-century European and colonial scene, illustrations such as the following, which now appear nothing more than charming curiosities:

"In North America, provisions are much cheaper and wages much higher than in England. In the province of New York, common labourers earn 3/6d. currency, equal to 2/- sterling a day."

"A middling farmer in France will sometimes have 400 fowls in his yard."

"The South Sea Company never had any forts or garrisons to maintain, and therefore were entirely exempted from one great expense, to which other joint stock companies for foreign trade are subject."

What of the economic message? The book was hailed primarily as a powerful challenge to the prevailing restrictive spirit of Mercantilism. The last treatise on political economy published in England had been written by Smith's contemporary, Sir James Steuart. His book, *The Principles of Political Economy*, published in 1767, was at this time a respected and widely consulted piece of work. An extract from some of its principles will show what Adam Smith was up against. On the presumption that foreign trade is mischievous, Steuart had argued that it should be treated under the three following principles:

> That in a country entirely taken up with the object of foreign trade, no competition should be allowed to come from abroad for articles of the first necessity, and princpally for food, so as to raise prices beyond a certain standard.
>
> That no domestic competition should be encouraged upon articles of superfluity, so as to raise prices beyond a certain standard.
>
> That when these standards cannot be preserved, and that, from natural causes, prices get above them, public money must be thrown into the scale to bring prices to the level of those of exportation. The greater the extent of foreign trade in any

nation is, the lower these standards *must* be kept;
the less the extent of it is, the higher they may be
allowed to rise.

Considering the subject in a broad way, Steuart had concluded: "It is a general maxim to discourage the importation
of work, and to encourage the exportation of it. . . ."

In a letter to Pulteney in 1772, Smith wrote: "I have the
same opinion of Sir James Steuart's book that you have.
Without once mentioning it, I flatter myself that any falla-
cious principle in it will meet with a clear and distinct con-
futation in mine." Smith did indeed confute. Moreover, he
did not confine himself to foreign trade but bombarded protectionism in *all* its varieties. Apprenticeships, medical licensing systems, universities, trading companies (like the
East India), in fact all eighteenth-century institutions that
were steeped in the spirit of monopoly fell victims to his
attack.

But *The Wealth of Nations* is not remembered chiefly for
its eighteenth-century illustrations and curiosities; it is, of
course, recognized as a classic work in economic thought.
The work had its polemical aspects, it is true. But at the same
time it was an original attempt to produce a comprehensive
economic system, a system, moreover, which could be understood by wide sections of the reading public. The announced object of the book was the analysis of the social
causes which determined the real national income per head.
Smith had already elicited several of these causes (as we have
seen) in his Glasgow lectures. In *The Wealth of Nations* they
are worked up with much more thoroughness and into a
more rounded and comprehensive form.

Of the major causes of increasing wealth of nations—and
the term "wealth" Smith in fact implied not a *stock* (of cap-

ital) but a *flow* (of national income) over a period of time—pride of place is given, as in the lectures, to the division of labor. The opening sentence of the very first chapter states: "The greatest improvement in the productive powers of labour, and the greater part of the skill, dexterity and judgement with which it is anywhere directed, or applied, seem to have been the effects of the division of labour." This first chapter, which is probably one of the most polished pieces of the whole work, provides the clearest exposition ever given of the reasons why the division of labor increases productivity. The division of labor included not only occupational specialization within an enterprise, but also specialization between firms. The idea eventually embraced the full sweep of "social division of labour" envisaging the whole society split up into specialist parts, including some, such as invention, which provided the springs of technical progress.

In the second chapter Smith considered the engine by which this whole edifice was constructed, namely, mutual exchange, which was stimulated by the human propensity to truck, barter and exchange. Chapter III shows how the division of labor is limited by the extent of the market. As productivity and exchange increased, the market was facilitated by the use of money. This is discussed in Chapter IV. The use of money, in turn, led into the problems of value or pricing, which are discussed in Chapters V to VII.

In these chapters Smith groped with crude analytical tools on a problem upon which much advance has been made since his time. He discussed the two questions of the *measure* of value and the *determination* of value. In Chapter V of Book I he used as an index of welfare a "labour-command" standard to measure long-run real income. Each man was better off the more he could avoid irksome labor and impose it on others; his desire for such transfer of effort encouraged the use of the division of labor; the ultimate standard of wealth was the amount of other people's labor he purchased with it in the market. Marx was later to argue that Smith here made a confused attempt at a labor theory of value. This is largely an erroneous interpretation, however. There is a crucial difference between using someting as an *index* of value and arguing that this same "something" is the sole *cause* of value.

Chapters VI and VII of Book I, in fact, outlined not a labor theory but a (total) cost of production theory of value (a theory whose chief defect, of course, is its neglect of the function of demand). In the long run, Smith argued, the natural price of an article was the sum of all the amounts payable to *all* the factors used in making it—wages, rents and profits. He seems to have been at pains to reject the labor cost theory of value so widespread among his predecessors. It was wrong, he insisted, to treat the "profits of stock" as only "a different name for the wage of a particular sort of labour." Many stock (i.e., capital) owners did not participate personally in management, yet each of them demanded profits in "regular proportion to his capital."

> In the price of commodities, therefore, the profits of stock constitute a component part altogether different from the wages of labour, and regulated by quite different principles.
>
> In this state of things, the whole produce of labour does not always belong to the labourer. He must in most cases share it with the owner of the stock which employs him. (I. p. 53)

Smith's new attempt to grope through to a solution of how

production and valuation took place simultaneously with the distribution of the national product among the owners of the factors of production was an important innovation. A theory of the distribution of factor shares did not appear in the Glasgow Jurisprudence Lectures of the 1750s. According to Dugald Stewart, however, Smith told him in 1755 that he was much indebted to James Oswald (mentioned above, p. 45) for this new "discovery." An elementary theory of distribution did appear also in an early draft of *The Wealth of Nations* written in the early 1760s, prior to Smith's continental tour. (See W. R. Scott, *Adam Smith As Student and Professor*, 1937, pp. 117 and 320.) Smith examined wages in *The Wealth of Nations* in Chapter VIII, and then profits in Chapter IX. In a classic Chapter X (which is still prescribed reading on this subject) he analyzed the causes of the differences in earnings between different employments of labor and capital. Although Smith neglected the demand side of his wage theory, on the supply side it was a significant pioneering development. The upshot of his analysis was that competition equalized the sum of the pecuniary and non-pecuniary returns (the "net advantages") of different occupations. Each individual reward was weighted by the following five considerations: attractiveness of the work, the cost of acquiring the necessary skill, the regularity or seasonality of employment, the degree of responsibility necessary for the job, and finally the probability or improbability of success in it. Referring to the last of these, Smith called attention to the way in which certain professions had become overcrowded because of the "over-weaning conceit which the greater part of men have of their own activities" and "their absurd presumption in their own good fortune." Chapter XI of *The Wealth of Nations* completed the analysis of the rewards to agents of production by looking at rent and the influence of the progress of the economy upon the distribution of the product between landlords, wage earners, merchants and master-manufacturers.

As the division of labor progressed, so did the significance of capital. In Book II, therefore, Smith discussed this factor in five separate chapters whose interrelationship is explained in a short introduction. The accumulation of capital was a necessary condition for economic progress. When the division of labor had been thoroughly established, each man depended for most of his necessities upon the labor of others. Since such production now took much time before it was finally sold on the market, a stock of goods of different kinds, including tools and materials, had to be stored up sufficiently to maintain each participant until such a time as his own productive contribution in the joint venture came to fruition. The person who "employs his stock in maintaining labour" necessarily wished to employ it "so as to produce as great a quantity of work as possible" and to provide them with the best machines. Smith then implied what modern economics calls a "capital output ratio."

> His abilities in both these respects are generally in proportion to the extent of his stock or to the number of people whom it can employ. The quantity of industry, therefore, not only increases in every country with the increase of the stock which employs it, but, in consequence of that increase, the same quantity of industry produces a much greater quantity of work. (I. p. 294)

In the same Book, Smith examined money and banking. The chief function of banks, Smith insisted, should be to administer the use of paper money in strict proportions to available precious metals so as to economize the latter. "The substitution of paper in the room of gold and silver money," he wrote, "replaces a very expensive instrument of commerce with one much less costly, and sometimes equally convenient." (I. p. 311) The anti-mercantilist monetary theory that Smith employed in the Glasgow lectures reappears in *The Wealth*. He was anxious to play down the notion that money was of any ultimate "real" significance in economic deliberation, a notion that paved the way for mercantilist trade restrictions. Smith the economic analyst was here somewhat dominated by Smith the free trade polemicist.[1]

In Chapter III of Book II Smith introduced his famous distinction between productive and unproductive labor. Although subsequently this has been much misinterpreted, Smith simply intended by it the analytic distinction between production which resulted in capital accumulation and activities which, like the services of the menial servant, "perish in the instant of their performance." Smith was distinguishing the second sort of labor, not belittling it. "The labour of the latter, however, has its value, and deserves its reward as well as that of the former."

Yet Smith, like a prudent steward of a Scottish aristocrat's estate, could hardly disguise a strong personal preference for much private frugality, and therefore for "productive labor," in the interests of the nation's future accumulation. In the *Moral Sentiments* (Part IV, Chapter II) frugality is a strong element of propriety and commands the esteem of the impartial spectator. "The spectator does not feel the solicitations of our present appetites. To him the pleasure which we are to enjoy a week hence, or a year hence, is just as interesting as that which we are to enjoy this moment." Now, in *The*

Wealth of Nations: when a nation was compared between two periods and it was observed that its annual produce had increased, we may be sure that its capital also must have increased ". . . and that more must have been added to it by the good conduct of some, than had been taken from it either by the private misconduct of others, or by the public extravagance of government." (I. p. 368) In peacetime, countries usually enjoyed economic growth *in spite of* governments! "But though the profusion of government must, undoubtedly, have retarded the natural progress of England towards wealth and improvement, it has not been able to stop it." (I. p. 370) England had enjoyed continuous saving and therefore steady growth for the whole previous century.

In Book III, Smith discussed "the different progress of opulence in different nations" and insisted how, despite the mutual and reciprocal gains that were to be obtained by the division of labor, the latter was frequently frustrated by absurd government policies and ancient systems of law. The primary example of policy which so hindered economic progress was that of the system of mercantilism. The main attack on this system was made in Book IV. This Book also had a chapter on the system of political economy as espoused by the economists of France (the physiocrats) and under the leadership of Quesnay, whom Smith had met on his Continental tour. Smith declared how impressed he was by the ingenuity of their system but had to reject it in view of its errors. The "capital error" was that it claimed agriculture to be the sole source of wealth and "artificers" to be altogether unproductive.

Erudite, encyclopaedic and discursive as it was, what distinguished *The Wealth* was, to repeat, the grand "orchestration" of parts into one central and systematic work. Strikingly novel too were many of the parts themselves, or at least so was the manner in which they were presented. Consider, for instance, the chapters upon taxation in the final Book, V. Today they still find a classic place in most textbooks on public finance. They read as follows:

1. The subjects of every State should contribute (tax revenue) in proportion to their respective abilities.
2. The tax which each individual is bound to pay ought to be certain, and not arbitrary.
3. Every tax ought to be levied at the time, or in the manner, in which it is most likely to be convenient for the contributor to pay it.
4. Every tax ought to be so contrived as both to take out and to keep out of the pockets of the people as little as possible, over and above what it brings into the public treasury and the state.

Smith did not, of course, *enthuse* about taxes. Indeed, more often than not he treated them as one of the important hindrances to prosperity. His opposition, however, was directed mainly towards *excessive* taxes, taxes raised to provide revenue for scandalously wasteful and unnecessary public expenditure. Some public expenditure, he acknowledged, was of course essential. Defense, law and order, roads, and some finance for education—all these and more were recognized to be legitimate areas in the public sector. Revenue for such obligations was indeed necessary; but the requisite taxation should nevertheless conform to his "canons."

Smith's views on the national debt and unbalanced budgets in particular revealed the full vigor of his opposition to mercantilists like Steuart. In issuing debt, governments deprived industry and commerce of capital and thereby caused an increase of present consumption. This was to the detriment of accumulation and growth. Unbalanced budgets were a menace to liberty. Once the sovereign developed a taste for borrowing he would realise an increase in his political power since he would no longer be so dependent on tax exactions. Such borrowing would lead him into costly and unnecessary wars. If wars had to be financed from taxes they would in general "be more speedily concluded, and less wantonly undertaken."

Now, in the very last chapter of *The Wealth of Nations*, Smith's style had reached its zenith, with literary elegance perfectly blended with pungent argument. The "ruinous practice" of perpetual funding to meet government emergencies he roundly condemned in the following terms:

> To relieve the present exigency is always the object which principally interests those immediately concerned in the administration of public affairs. The future liberation of the public revenue, they leave to the care of posterity. (II. p. 534)

The proposition that the national debt is not really a burden to the country but only an *internal* transfer was in Smith's time a prominent mercantilist argument. (It has since been revived in the subsequent era of "Keynesian economics.")[2] Smith dispensed with it thus:

> In the payment of the interest of the public debt, it has been said, it is the right hand which pays the left. The money does not go out of the country. It is only a part of the revenue of one set of the inhabitants which is transfered to another; and the nation is not a farthing the poorer. This apology is founded altogether in the sophistry of the mercan-

tile system, and after the long examination which I
have already bestowed upon that system, it may
perhaps be unnecessary to say any thing further
about it. (I. p. 548)

Smith went on to explain that because the taxes impover-
ished the private sources of revenue, land and capital stock,
this led to the withdrawal of capital from the country by
owners who had become irritated with "the mortifying and
vexatious visits of the tax-gatherers."

Prodigious as *The Wealth of Nations* is, it is astonishing to
remember that it was conceived as a part of a much larger
work. In the concluding paragraph of *The Theory of Moral
Sentiments* (first published in 1759) Smith had promised: "I
shall in another discourse endeavour to give an account of
the general principles of law and government, and of the
different revolutions they have undergone in the different
ages and periods of society, not only in what concerns justice,
but in what concerns policy, revenue and arms, and whatever
else is the object of law." In the preface of the sixth edition of
The Theory, written in the last year of his life, Smith explained that in *The Wealth* he had "partially executed this
promise, at least so far as concerns policy, revenue and arms."
In the course of a scheme of vast research "far surpassing the
means at his disposal, and too good for any single man. . . ,"
Smith, according to one writer, "came upon *The Wealth of
Nations*, for dealing with which his powers and his opportunities peculiarly fitted him, and on that he wrote a book,
which has itself deeply influenced thought and policy which
has been the beginning of a new science." Smith was "like
Saul, who went in search of his father's asses and found a
kingdom."[3]

But it would be wrong to conclude that Smith's *The

Wealth of Nations superseded and overshadowed his previous work. This certainly does not seem to have been the opinion of Smith himself, who, after the publication of *The Wealth*, continued zealously to edit new editions of *The Theory of Moral Sentiments*. *The Wealth of Nations* did indeed contain the new and brilliant economic insight and wisdom; nevertheless, there are clear and important links with the earlier philosophical work.

We have already examined the opinion that Smith's first book presents the view of a beatific state where private actions are directed by an Invisible Hand to bring society into Natural Harmony. What of this same kind of summary judgemeant which is often made also of *The Wealth of Nations?* Certainly Smith spoke in terms of an "obvious and simple system of natural liberty" which often led to the reconciling of private with social interests. There is in this book, however, unlike its predecessor the *Moral Sentiments*, no "personification in theological shape." It would appear to the modern reader that the kind of "harmony" or "balance" that Smith was pointing to was not a theological but a scientific phenomenon. Other sciences today unselfconsciously study the formation of spontaneous or self-determining orders without concerning themselves about possible connections with Deistic design. Indeed, natural scientists are now in the 1960's acknowledging Smith's "invisible hand" methodology as a pioneering use of the idea of cybernetics, free market prices being seen as regulated by "negative feedback."[4] Smith himself certainly did not speak as though men were *actually* led by, but only *as if by*, an "invisible hand"; the metaphor, in other words, was a useful way of formulating a testable hypothesis. The modern economist notices, incidentally, that Smith's self-regulating mechanism was seen by him not primarily as a means of achieving a static "optimum" distribution of resources, but rather as a dynamic means of widening markets, developing the division of labor and promoting growth.

As in the Glasgow lectures, so in *The Wealth of Nations*, Smith did not look at the free market system in abstraction but only in the context of an appropriate legal framework and one wherein government had definite functions. The latter included especially the provision of military security, the administration of justice and "the duty of erecting and maintaining certain public works and certain public institutions, which it can never be for the interest of any individual or small number of individuals, to erect and maintain; because the profit could neither repay the expense to any individual or small number of individuals, though it may frequently do much more than repay it to a great society." (I. p. 325) In other words, Smith searched pragmatically for those institutions which were not appropriate under given circumstances. Market forces would only be beneficial under some of these circumstances and there was no doctrinaire line to be drawn. Smith was aware, for instance, that one can have a price system without a "laissez faire" free market. He made scrupulous examination, in fact, of the circumstances where one was more suitable than the other, or where it was better to have a mixture of both. Thus he maintained that in public education government should subsidize the school buildings, whereas a good part of the schoolmaster's salary should come out of private fees. Highways, bridges, canals and harbors should be financed partly out of user prices (tolls), and partly out of a general or local tax revenue. Canals were less adapted to "nationalization" than roads, since their owners had substantial incentives to maintain them.

In the last few pages of *The Wealth of Nations*, Smith discussed the current Irish and American problems. The appropriate solution to these great questions required, he maintained, the counsel of the best philosophers, legislators and statesmen. We know from *The Theory of Moral Sentiments* that Smith was on his guard against "that insidious and crafty animal, vulgarly called a statesman or politician whose councils are directed by the monetary fluctuations of affairs." The same book shows also, however, Smith's hope that there could be found another type of statesman who was concerned not with "momentary fluctuations of affairs" but with the long-run interests of his people, and Smith's belief in noble statesmen as well as "crafty" ones. Of a status that was even higher than that of noble statesmen was the scientific legislator whose deliberations were governed by the highest and most constant principles. This person, whose virtue was a reflection of the guidance of the most refined Impartial Spectator, could make all the difference between success and failure, between happiness and misery. Although success was far from inevitable (and here Smith cuts himself off sharply from the French philosophers) it was the clear duty of those whose thoughts were prompted by the deepest reflection to lay them before their countrymen in the hopes that their words would one day be heeded.

It was in this vein that Smith set forth his views on the American question in the final chapter of *The Wealth of Nations*. The extension of the British system of taxation to all the different provinces of the Empire could scarcely be done, he argued, "consistently with the principles of the British constitution, without admitting into the British parliament . . . a fair and equal representation of all those different provinces, that of each province bearing the same proportion to the produce of its taxes, as the representation of Great Britain might bear to the produce of the taxes levied upon Great Britain."

> The private interest of many powerful individuals, the confirmed prejudices of great bodies of people seem, indeed, at present, to oppose to so great a change such obstacles as it may be very difficult, perhaps altogether impossible, to surmount. Without, however, pretending to determine whether such a union be practicable or impracticable, it may not, perhaps, be improper, in a speculative work of this kind, to consider how far the British system of taxation might be applicable to all the different provinces of the Empire; what revenue might be expected from it if so applied, and in what manner a general union of this kind might be likely to affect the happiness and prosperity of the different provinces comprehended within it. Such a speculation can at worst be regarded but as a new Utopia, less amusing certainly, but not more useless and chimerical than the old one. (II. p. 556)

Smith goes on to show that the American plantations were more able to pay a land tax than Great Britain. Stamp duties could be applied to all countries *so long as their legal structures were on an equal footing*. The extension of the custom-house laws of Great Britain to America would be in the highest degree advantageous to both, *provided:* "it was accompanied, as in justice it ought to be, with an extension of the freedom of trade. . . . The trade between all the different parts of the British Empire would, in consequence of this uniformity in the custom-house laws, be as free as the coasting trade of Great Britain is at present. The British Empire would thus afford within itself an immense internal market for every part of the produce of all its different provinces." (II. p. 557) The difficulties in the way of a union were not, argued Smith, insurmountable. And what difficulties did exist arose ". . . not from the nature of things, but from the prejudice and opinions both on this and on the other side of the Atlantic." He recognized that Americans were afraid that the distance from the seat of government might damage their interests. He reminded them, however, that their representatives in parliament ". . . of which the number ought from the very first to be considerable" were, in his scheme, to be in proportion to the produce of American taxation. As he expected American produce and population to continue to rise as it had done in the past, in the course of about a century the produce of America might exceed that of British taxation. "The seat of the Empire would then naturally remove itself to that part of the Empire which contributed most to the general defense and support of the whole." Such was Adam Smith's vision—an Anglo-American empire with its capital on the other side of the Atlantic! Too Utopian? But what were the alternatives then being discussed? Force did not solve anything. ". . . They are very weak who flatter themselves that, in the state to which things have come, our colonies will be easily conquered by force alone. . . . No oppressive aristocracy has ever prevailed in the colonies."

How fatuous to believe that Britain could continue to keep America "as a sort of splendid and showy equipage of the Empire." The whole thing had become far too costly; the moment of truth had arrived.

The rulers of Great Britain have, for more than a century past, amused the people with the imagination that they possessed a great Empire on the west side of the Atlantic. This Empire, has however, hitherto existed in imagination only. It has hitherto been, not an Empire, but the project of an Empire; not a gold-mine, but the project of a gold-mine; a project which has cost, which continues to cost, and which if pursued in the same way as it has been hitherto, is likely to cost, immense expense, without being likely to bring any profits; for the effects of the monopoly of the colony trade, it has been shown, are, to the great body of the people, mere loss instead of profit.

The British government was no longer in charge of the situation; they were being forced by events. The rulers should properly and sensibly either at last realize their "golden dream" of Empire or awake from it. If the project could not be completed it ought to be abandoned. And characteristically the author of *The Wealth of Nations* ends his classic work with one imperious and deliberately challenging sentence, the sting of which is in the tail:

If any of the provinces of the British Empire cannot be made to contribute towards the support of the whole Empire, it is surely time that Great Britain should free herself from the expense of defending those provinces in time of war, and of supporting any part of their civil or military establishments in time of peace, *and endeavour to accommodate her future views and designs to the real mediocrity of her circumstances.* (II. p. 571; italics provided.)

It is possible that as Smith proceeded with his book, the subject of America became more and more of an obsession with him. At first sight it appears that the huge section of the book, (Book IV), on the mercantile system is out of balance with the rest. If, however, we compare it with Books II and III which precede it, and with Book V which follows it, a pattern is clear to see. A vivid application of theory showing what are the true causes of the growth of the wealth of nations and what are the ideal conditions for the increase in prosperity is juxtaposed with a sorry picture of mercantilist Europe where these conditions had been frustrated by incompetent governments. The references to America in Books I, III and V, in contrast, present the hope of a new world where the true understanding of the virtues of free trade coupled with the republican spirit would at last set a true example to the world.

One may well wonder why America has not rejoiced in Adam Smith more than it has done. Sentiments of nationalism and self-determination no doubt could be offered as the obvious explanation. A stronger reason, however, is that after the Revolution, America did not really favor free trade anyway. The Boston Tea Party did not encourage the idea that import duties were inherently bad. The United States indeed, soon settled down to a strong policy of protection, influenced no doubt by Alexander Hamilton's *Report on the Subject of Manufactures* (1791). After the turn of the century there was a gradual piling up of tariffs so that by 1828, when the so called "Tariff of Abomination" was passed, they had indeed reached the height of 48 per cent. The United States, moreover, did not join in the European movement towards free trade after 1860 but remained the most protected country in the world for the rest of the 19th century.

The author of *The Wealth of Nations* would clearly have been disappointed. Judged by his criteria, affairs must have fallen into the hands, not of his scientific legislator "whose deliberations ought to be governed by general principles which are always the same," but into those of that "insidious and crafty animal" who was "vulgarly called" a statesman or politician. But that was America in the nineteenth century. Purposeful domestic anti-trust activity in the twentieth century, together with the Kennedy Round at the international level, have both altered the picture substantially.

CHAPTER XIV

The Commissioner of Customs

THE ideas for *new* taxes in *The Wealth of Nations* were discussed in the context of improving the system of public finance as a whole; besides new taxes to be established, there were old ones to be abolished. Smith had confined his attention mainly to the question: Assuming that a government is determined to raise a *given total* of expenditure, what were the best means of raising the revenue? The question was not how can the government get more money to spend, but how could existing taxation be modified so as to achieve minimum hurt to the public? The tax on manservants, on property sold by auction, the inhabited-house duty and the malt tax were all put forward by Smith in this context. In the wartime emergency, however, Lord North eagerly seized upon these ideas in the pursuit of increased *total* revenue. To the author of *The Wealth of Nations*, the man of peace and friend of America, this outcome must have seemed poignant indeed.

But there was even more irony in an accompanying event. Smith, the eloquent champion of free trade, was offered the post of Commissioner of Customs in Scotland, an employment which involved the collection of those customs and tariffs which he had worked so hard to condemn! The most tempting aspect of the offer, which brought the handsome income of £600 per year, was that it would enable Smith to settle at last among his friends and relations and in the neighborhood of his birth and upbringing. His mother, who was now suffering ill health, would be enabled to come the few miles from Kirkcaldy and stay with him in the comfort of a new house in Edinburgh. Some attributed the offer to the influence of the Duke of Buccleugh (his old pupil) and to Henry Dundas, then Lord Advocate for Scotland. Others, however, believed that the appointment was really a direct reward to the author of *The Wealth of Nations* for contributing so effectively to government policy. Whatever the indirect influences, the direct responsibility for the appointment rested upon Lord North.

Most paradoxes, however, can be resolved. Smith's proposal was not that customs and tariffs should be totally abolished; his chief complaints concerned the arbitrary, unpredictable nature in which they were imposed, the high costs of collection and their manipulation in favor of monopolies and special interest groups. To enter the service of the Customs would not be to compromise his principles. On the contrary he would be enabled more practically to study further ways of achieving economies. It is interesting that after seven years in office he wrote to William Eden: "It may perhaps give that gentleman [Mr. Rose of the Treasury] pleasure to be informed that the net revenue arising from the Customs of Scotland is at least four times greater than it was seven or eight years ago. It has been increasing rapidly these four or five years past, and the revenue of this year has over-leaped by at least one half the revenue of the greatest former year. I flatter myself it is likely to increase still further." Smith was emphasizing an increase in the *net* revenue, and one of the most important causes of this was the reduction in the costs of collection during Smith's period of office.

After Smith's acceptance of the Customs post in 1778 he settled in Edinburgh, taking a house in the Canongate. This building, Panmure House, which still stands today, was to be his home for the remaining twelve years of his life. There he was joined by his mother and his cousin, Miss Douglas, and later he took in the youngest son of Colonel Douglas of Strathendry, his cousin. Every day Commissioner Smith was a familiar figure walking along the Canongate towards the Custom House in Exchange Square off the High Street. At the Custom House he shared his duties with four other Commissioners. The business would have included a miscellany of duties such as the consideration of appeals from merchants against local assessments, a plan for a new lighthouse, an examination of a petition from a wine importer, investigations of reports of illicit trading in the locality, the dispatching of troops to repress illegal distilleries and the making of annual returns of income and expenditure to the Treasury.

In his book Smith had argued that where customs were excessive the law always fell into disrepute. He showed sympathy with the ordinary people's frustration with excessive government restrictions and shared their outrage at signs of corruption. Indeed, in his opinion, it was not always immoral under such circumstances to buy smuggled goods. To have any scruple, "though a manifest encouragement of the violation of the revenue laws," would be regarded in most places as being a "pedantic piece of hypocrisy." The person who complained would be under the suspicion of "being a greater knave than most of his neighbours." As Commissioner of

Customs it was now Adam Smith's duty to listen to such complaints and to pursue the illegal traffickers. Such a position could only be free from hypocrisy on his own part if he thought, as he obviously did, that his ordinary job of policing the revenue could be augmented by that of assisting custom reform. Nevertheless there must have been many perturbing experiences, especially in the early days when events like the following had to be recorded: "Scottish Customs. Thursday July 23rd, 1778. Adam Smith in the chair. Was horrified to find that McPhie [a customs officer] was 'in the pay of the smugglers'."[1]

The post involved heavy routine work no doubt, but it obviously had its excitements too. Indeed, at one point there was a dramatic reminder of the American War which was now in full progress. In September, 1779, the following anxious letter bearing Smith's signature with others went out from the Custom House at Kirkcaldy:

> We have received yours of the 14th inst., by express relative to three Privateers and a Frigate supposed to be French, being off the coast of Dunbar and Eyemouth and also your letter dated the 15th, at 1 o'clock noon, signifying that four vessels were then standing with their heads to the northward about 24 miles off Dunbar which it is believed are enemy ships; and we command your attention hereon; and have communicated the intelligence to the Commander in Chief, and to the Commander of His Majesty's ships in the Firth. Your loving friends, Adam Smith, George Maxwell, Paul Cochrane.

The enemy raiding squadron was in fact being led by none other than Paul Jones, the Scottish-born founder of the

United States Navy. The squadron, which consisted of United States and French ships, was making havoc of British shipping coming southward down the eastern seaboard of Scotland. Jones's ships—"Bonhomme Richard," "Alliance" and "Palace Vengeance"—entered the Firth of Forth on the 14th of September with the purpose of forcing a ransom of £200,000 from the Port of Leith. Accurate intelligence of the Forth defenses was given to Paul Jones by a captured Kirkcaldy skipper, Andrew Robertson. On Sunday the 17th, large crowds gathered on the beach where the Reverend Shirra prayed on the sands for a wind to blow Paul Jones out of the Forth. Eventually a violent gale did come up with sudden fury and Paul Jones's ships were forced to leave the Firth.[2]

When the American "problem" temporarily slipped from view there was always that of the Irish. In 1779 Lord Carlisle, head of the Board of Trade, applied to Smith (through their common friend Adam Ferguson) for advice on the Irish question. (Lord Carlisle, incidentally, had been President and Ferguson Secretary of the Commission which had been sent out to America the year before to negotiate the terms of peace.) At the same time, Mr. William Eden, Secretary of the Board of Trade, also sought Smith's advice through Henry Dundas. The Irish were at this time being cruelly oppressed by commercial restrictions imposed by the English government. Forbidden to trade as they would with Great Britain and her colonies because they were aliens, the Irish were not allowed to trade as they wanted to with foreign countries because they were British subjects. The moment they tried to export commodities in which they had a clear advantage, Parliament would close the market against them. As Rae puts it: "When stopped from sending live meat, they tried to send dead, but the embargo was promptly extended to salt provisions. Driven from cattle, they betook themselves to sheep, and sent over wool; that was stopped, allowed, and stopped again. When their raw wool was denied a market, they next tried cloth, but England then bargained for the suppression of the chief branches of Irish woollen manufacture by promising Ireland a monopoly of the manufacture of linen."[3] Rebellion was brewing, the Irish were refusing to pay taxes and many of them had gone as recruits to the revolutionary army in America. The Irish Protestants had even raised an illegal army of 42,000 volunteers.

In his advice to Lord Carlisle, Smith first reviewed the facts of the situation. He pointed out that the Irish were forbidden to export glass to any country at all and that they only exported wool to Great Britain. Moreover, they could only export woolen manufactures from certain ports in Ireland to certain ports in Great Britain. After the facts comes the analysis. It is sharp, pungent and barbed: "A very slender interest of our own manufactures is the foundation of all these unjust and oppressive restraints. The watchful jealousy of those gentlemen is alarmed least the Irish, who never have been able to supply completely even their own market with glass or woollen manufactures, should be able to rival them in foreign markets." Smith reminded Lord Carlisle that the Irish could import glass, sugars of foreign plantations (except those of Spain or Portugal) and certain kinds of East India goods from no country but Britain. "The Irish probably mean to demand no more than this most just and reasonable freedom of exportation and importation; in restraining which we seem to me rather to have gratified the impertinence than to have promoted any solid interest of our merchants and manufacturers." On the possibility of the Irish exporting to Britain, Smith gave the following verdict: ". . . I cannot believe that the interests of Britain would be hurt by it. On the contrary, the competition of Irish goods in the British market might contribute to break down in part that monopoly which we have most absurdly granted to the greater part of our own workmen against ourselves. . . . Should the industry of Ireland, in consequence of freedom and good government, ever equal that of England, so much the better would it be not only for the whole British Empire, but for the particular province of England. As the wealth and industry of Lancashire does not obstruct but promote that of Yorkshire, so the wealth and industry of Ireland would not obstruct but promote that of England." In those days Ireland was the English businessman's "Japan." The expressed fear was that it would unfairly compete against them by exploiting cheap labor resources. That, however, is what free trade is all about; and Commissioner Smith told them so.

In his letter to Smith, Henry Dundas observed:

> . . . it has long appeared to me that the bearing down of Ireland was in truth bearing down a substantial part of the Naval and Military strength of our own Country. Indeed, it has often shocked me in the House of Commons for these two years past, when anything was hinted in favour of Ireland by friends of giving them only the benefit of making the most of what their soil and climate afforded them to hear it received as a sufficient answer that a town in England or Scotland would be hurt by such an Indulgence. This kind of reasoning will no longer do. But I find, in place of asking yours, I am giving you my opinion. Yours sincerely, Henry Dundas

Smith's instincts for liberty were keenly aroused. He knew,

however, that its cause was most shrewdly protected by emphasis upon self-interest. This was his reply to Dundas:

> I perfectly agree with your Lordship that to Crush the Industry of so great and so fine a Province of the Empire in order to favour the monopoly of some particular Towns in Scotland or England is equally injurious and impolitic. The general opulence and improvement of Ireland must certainly, under proper management, afford much greater resources to Government than can ever be drawn from a few mercantile or manufacturing Towns. . . . Nothing, in my opinion, would be more highly advantageous to both countries than this mutual freedom of trade. It would help to break down that absurd monopoly which we have most absurdly established against ourselves in favour of almost all the different Classes of our own manufacturers.

Playing another tactical card, Smith reminded Dundas that England was suffering an unprecedented strain in the unequal war against France, Spain and America. ". . . Whatever the Irish mean to demand in this way [i.e. free trade], in the present situation of our affairs I should think it madness not to grant it."

And finally, returning to the theme of self-interest, Smith's logic led him (consistently) to suggest something akin to "honest bribes," or what would be called in the smarter terminology of today's welfare economics "compensations."

> . . . Whatever they [the Irish] may demand, our manufacturers, unless the leading and principal men among them are properly dealt with beforehand, will probably oppose it. That they may be so

dealt with I know from experience, and that it may be done at little expense and with no great trouble. I could even point to some persons who, I think, are fit and likely to deal with them successfully for this purpose. I shall not say more upon this till I see you, which I shall do the first moment I get out of this Town.

The "true" lover of liberty values freedom for its own sake. The person who supports freedom only because it will have consequences that he approves of is not so committed. Smith was the "true" libertarian. True, he supported the idea of Irish freedom on the grounds of the favorable expected consequences for England; but this was mainly an expedient argument for the freedom he so obviously cherished for itself. One does not have to look hard through Smith's writings to find liberty treated as a value *absolute*. If utility (as he tells us in *The Theory of Moral Sentiments*) is not the primary foundation of ethics, neither is it of liberty. Again and again he reveals himself as an arch opponent of established oligarchies, entrenched aristocracies and oppressive religious establishments. In Ireland he found all three. *The Wealth of Nations* proclaimed:

By a union with Great Britain, Ireland would gain, besides the freedom of trade, other advantages much more important, and which would much more than compensate any increase of taxes that might accompany that union. By the union with England, the middling and inferior ranks of people in Scotland gained a complete deliverance from the power of an aristocracy which had always before oppressed them. By a union with Great Britain, the greater part of the people of all ranks in Ireland would gain an equally complete deliverance from a much more oppressive aristocracy; an aristocracy not founded, like that of Scotland, in the natural and respectable distinctions of birth and fortune; but in the most odious of all distinctions, those of religious and political prejudices; distinctions which, more than any other, animate both the insolence of oppressors and the hatred and indignation of the oppressed, and which commonly render the inhabitants of the same country more hostile to one another than those of different countries ever are. Without a union with Great Britain, the inhabitants of Ireland are not likely for many ages to consider themselves as one people. (II. p. 568)

Here was the exponent of the principle of natural liberty in full cry; here was the true architect of freedom using every opportunity, every tactic and every argument in a supreme cause.

The emancipation of people from the influence of overpowerful monarchies was another persistent Smithian theme in his grand campaign for liberty. His many differences with the French Physiocrats, incidentally, included a strong disagreement with their philosophy of trusting the implementation of their system of "perfect liberty" to the approval and protection of a great monarch. Whereas Quesnay's thought was for the power of the king as well as for the welfare of the people, Smith suspected the former and would include liberty in the latter. It is interesting too that statesmen such as Pitt and Shelburne, who were the most energetic in pursuing Smith's free trade policy, did not draw his political approval. The reason is that Shelburne's and Pitt's strong support of the king was, in Smith's view, a serious detriment to the House of Commons. Political liberty was more important to

him than the success of his economic policies. A Rockingham Whig, like his friend Edmund Burke, Smith at all times
stood for strengthening constitutional usages and curbing the
power of the monarch. Like Burke also, he wanted to pre-
serve those things that had stood the test of time; change
should be gradual, not radical. Moreover, he was a patriot.
When he was brought the news of Saratoga in 1778, his
young messenger, John Sinclair, declared that the nation
must be ruined. "Be assured, my young friend," Smith replied, "there is a great deal of ruin in a nation."

Visiting Edinburgh in 1782, Sir Gilbert Eliot wrote to his
wife:

> I have found one just man in Gomorrah, Adam
> Smith, author of *The Wealth of Nations*. He was
> the Duke of Buccleugh's tutor, is a wise and deep
> philosopher, and although made Commissioner of
> the Customs here by the Duke and Lord Advocate,
> is what I call an *honest fellow*. He wrote a most
> kind as well as elegant letter to Burke on his resig-
> nation, as I believe I told you before, and on my
> mentioning it to him he told me that he was the
> only man here who spoke out for the Rocking-
> hams.

His political opinion notwithstanding, Pitt always declared
himself as one of the most convinced of Smith's disciples on
questions of economics. In 1787, having achieved a measure
of commercial emancipation for Ireland and the great Commercial Treaty with France, he undertook one of the most
thoroughgoing pieces of legislation of all times concerning
the collection and administration of the revenue. Pitt's great
Consolidation Bill, which was based fully on Smithian prin-

ciple, was designed to create order out of the chaos of ancient customs and excise regulations. A total of 2,537 separate resolutions was required to present the provisions of this Bill, which was going through Parliament when Smith made his last visit to London in this year, 1787, three years before his death.

During this visit Smith was often at the Ministry, and the clerks of the public offices had orders to furnish him with all papers and to employ additional assistants, if necessary, to copy for him. During this same visit also he was the frequent personal guest of Pitt. On one occasion, at a meeting at Henry Dundas' house, there were present among others, Addington, Wilberforce and Grenville. Legend has it that when Smith, who was one of the last guests to arrive, entered the room, the whole company rose from their seats to receive him. When Commissioner Smith requested, "Be seated, gentlemen", Pitt replied, "No sir, we will stand till you are first seated, for we are all your scholars."

But the teacher had grown old and his health was in decline. He went back home to Edinburgh and the capital was to see him no more.

CHAPTER XV

Last Days

DURING the last years of Adam Smith's life, Edinburgh was clearly proud to count among its citizens such an eminent man of letters who was having so much influence upon the destiny of his own and other countries. The personal descriptions we have of him at this time clearly indicate that Smith, who experienced the infirmities of old age very early, had become even more of an eccentric. The picture by now could be straight out of Hogarth or Rowlandson. Every day he would be seen walking to the Customs House in a light-colored coat, probably linen, knee-breeches, white silk stockings, buckle shoes, and a flat broad-brimmed beaver hat. He would often be walking erect with a bunch of flowers in his left hand, and his cane, held by the middle, born on his right shoulder. His contemporary, Smellie, says that when he walked his head always moved gently from side to side and his body swayed as if at each alternate step "he meant to alter his direction, or even to turn back." Dugald Stewart tells us that "even in company, he was apt to be engrossed with his studies; and appeared, at times, by the motion of his lips, as well as by his looks and gestures, to be in the fervour of composition." Stewart charmingly defends Smith against any possible misinterpretation by saying that although he had many peculiarities which "were manifest to the most superficial observer" they did not detract in the slightest from the respect of his friends, to whom indeed they were a simple demonstration of "the artless simplicity of his heart."

In Stewart's opinion, Adam Smith was "certainly not fitted to the general commerce of the world." What an abundance of clerical mistakes at the Customs Office there must have been! One error at least is recorded. One day, having to sign an official document as Commissioner, Smith wrote an imitation of the signature of the Commissioner who had written before him instead of signing his own name! The most colorful story of all, however, comes to us from Sir Walter Scott. The Board of Customs had in their service a porter who, dressed in a huge scarlet gown or cloak "covered with frogs of worsted lace," would stand with a staff about seven feet high in his hand on guard outside the Custom House, whenever a Board was to be held. "It was the etiquette that as each Commissioner entered the porter should go through a sort of salute with his staff of office, resembling that which officers used formerly to perform through their spontoon, and then marshal the dignitary to the hall of meeting. Hundreds of times this ceremony must have been performed before Adam Smith without any incident. One day, however, on approaching the Customs House . . . the motions of this janitor seemed to have attracted his eye without their character or purpose reaching his apprehension, and on a sudden he began to imitate gestures as a recruit does those of his drill sergeant. The porter having drawn up in front of the door, presented his staff as a soldier does his musket. The Commissioner, raising his cane and holding it with both hands in the middle, returned the salute with the utmost gravity. The inferior officer, much annoyed, levelled his weapon, wheeled to the right, stepping a pace back to give the Commissioner room to pass, lowering his staff at the same time in token of obeisance. Dr. Smith instead of passing on, drew up on the opposite side and lowered his cane to the same angle. The functionary, much out of consequence, next moved upstairs with his staff upraised, while the author of *The Wealth of Nations* followed with his bamboo in precisely the same posture, and his whole soul apparently wrapped in the purpose of placing his foot on the same spot of each step which had been occupied by the officer who preceded him. At the door of the hall the porter again drew off, saluted with his staff, and bowed reverentially. The philosopher again imitated his motions, and returned his bow with the most profound gravity. Apparently when Smith was at last in the meeting chamber he came out of his spell. But one of his friends who had witnessed the whole performance had the greatest difficulty in convincing him that he had been doing 'anything extraordinary.' "[1]

With few exceptions Smith's companions showed the most sincere affection for him. He returned the affection of friends in full measure. Always a person of the highest integrity, Smith was a man of the staunchest loyalty to his close friends. The clearest example is his relationship with David Hume. After Hume's death, Smith wrote a warm-hearted eulogy of his friend which included the words, "Upon the whole, I have always considered him both in his lifetime and since his death as approaching as nearly to the idea of a perfectly wise and virtuous man, as perhaps the nature of human frailty will permit." Such a pronouncement brought considerable wrath upon Smith—especially from the church authorities, who were opposed to any praise of "heathens," however virtuous. According to Rae, Smith's words "rang like a challenge to religion itself."

Another friend for whom Smith showed similar constancy of feeling was Edmund Burke. In the first edition of *The Wealth of Nations* in 1776 Smith had criticized legislation, for which Burke had been responsible, concerning export bounties. Smith first met Burke in 1777, and it is interesting to notice that the criticism is tempered in the 1778 edition of *The Wealth of Nations* by the following: "So far, therefore, this law seems to be inferior to the ancient system. With all its imperfections, however, we may perhaps say of it what was said of the laws of Solon, that, though not the best in itself, it is the best which the interests, prejudices and temper of the times would admit of. It may perhaps in due time prepare the way for a better."

Smith regarded Burke as ". . . the only man I ever knew who thinks on economic subjects exactly as I do, without any previous communications having passed between us." In 1783, when Burke paid a visit to Scotland, having been elected Lord Rector of the University of Glasgow, he was the constant guest of Adam Smith and other stalwart Whigs such as John Millar the professor of law, and the young economist Lord Maitland (afterwards Lord Lauderdale). Burke's visit coincided with a general election in which the Whigs were being overwhelmed. Smith consoled the company with the thought that things would improve in about two years. Burke good-naturedly replied: "I have already been in a minority nineteen years, and your two years, Mr. Smith, will make me twenty-one years and it will surely be high time for me then to be in my majority!"

Exceptional instances did occur where Smith's personal relationships with others were not entirely happy ones. The notable example is his acquaintanceship with Dr. Johnson. It is clear that the two men were not enamored of each other's personalities, Johnson regarding Smith as somewhat of "a dull dog," while Smith was convinced that Johnson suffered from periodic forms of insanity. To third parties, however, they did have some good things to say of each other's works. Smith reviewed Dr. Johnson's dictionary quite favorably in the *Edinburgh Review* (although he had some reservations) while Johnson defended Smith against the accusations that a scholar could have nothing useful to say on the subject of trade and commerce. Johnson, as we have seen, approved of Smith's dislike of blank verse. Adam Smith thought Johnson's style was generally heavy and pedantic but considered his Preface to Shakespeare to be "the most manly piece of criticism that was every published in any country."

Smith's passion for literature remained to the end. He spent much time in his library reading classical Greek scholars such as Sophocles and Euripides and he told a friend that re-acquaintance with the favorites of one's youth was the most grateful and soothing diversion of old age. At his death Smith left a library approaching 3,000 volumes, only one-fifth of which related to political economy and history, the residue consisting of literature, art, law, geography and philosophy.

It would not have been unexpected to find that the private life of this man of letters—living much in abstraction and, in some important respects, living out of sympathy with many of the opinions and practices of his time—became dull and gray as he approached old age. It would have been understandable too, if the grief which he felt at the loss of his dearest relatives withdrew him still more from society. Smith's mother died in 1784 and his cousin, Miss Douglas, in

1788. Dugald Stewart observes: "They had been the objects of his affection for more than sixty years; and in their society he had enjoyed, from his infancy, all that he ever knew of the endearments of a family." Although his grief was considerable, he bore it with equanimity and eventually regained his former cheerfulness. We are reminded of a passage in his *Theory of Moral Sentiments:*

> Are you in adversity? Do not mourn in the darkness of solitude, do not regulate your sorrow according to the indulgent sympathy of your intimate friends; return, as soon as possible, to the daylight of the world and of society.

Smith's love of good conversation also persisted to the end. An eminently "clubable" man all his life, he helped to found the Oyster Club in Edinburgh in 1784. A Parisian doctor wrote to Jeremiah Bentham, ". . . we have a club here which consists of nothing but philosophers," with ". . . a most enlightened, agreeable, cheerful, and social company." Black, the founder of modern chemistry, and Hutton, the pioneer of geology, were the two other founders of this Society. Another member observed that these three illustrious men had enlarged views and wide information, "without any of the stateliness which men of letters think it sometimes necessary to affect; . . . and as the sincerity of their friendship had never been darkened by the least shade of envy, it would be hard to find an example where everything favourable to good society was more perfectly united, and everything adverse more entirely excluded."

In 1787 Smith heard with "heart-felt joy" the news that he had been elected a Rector of Glasgow University. He responded as follows:

No man can own greater obligations to a Society than I do to the University of Glasgow. They educated me, they sent me to Oxford, soon after my return to Scotland they elected me one of their own members, and afterwards preferred me to another office to which the abilities and virtues of the never-to-be-forgotten Dr. Hutcheson had given a superior degree of illustration. The period of 13 years which I spent as a member of that Society, I remember as by far the most useful and therefore as by far the happiest and most honourable period of my life; and now, after three-and-twenty years' absence, to be remembered in so very agreeable a manner by my old friends and protectors gives me a heart-felt joy which I cannot easily express to you.

Always a hospitable man, Smith's house was constantly open to visitors, and his celebrated Sunday suppers were remembered in Edinburgh circles long after his death. On one Sunday evening in July, 1790, Smith found that he could not sit up with his friends as usual. Retiring to bed he took leave of them with the words, "I believe we must adjourn this meeting gentlemen to some other place." He died a few days later on July 17th and was buried in the Canongate churchyard, which is very close to Panmure House. His burial place is marked by an unostentatious monument.

His friends were indignant that his death made little stir at the time; but there were many more friends to come. Adam Smith was dead! Long live Free Trade! For as Bagehot has said, Smith's name can no more be dissociated from free trade than Homer's from the siege of Troy.

So long as the doctrines of protection exist—and

they seem likely to do so, as human interests are what they are, and human nature is what it is— Adam Smith will always be quoted as the great authority on Anti-Protectionism, as the man who first told the world the truth, so that the world could learn and believe it.

Notes

CHAPTER 1

1. Adam Smith, *The Wealth of Nations* (Arlington House, 1966), Volume II, pp. 74-75.

CHAPTER 2

1. The details in this paragraph are taken from W. R. Scott, *Adam Smith, as Student and Professor* (Jackson Son & Co., University of Glasgow, 1937).
2. See the Bibliography for reference to the Stewart biography.
3. These and other similar details are contained in C. R. Fay, *Adam Smith and the Scotland of his Day* (Cambridge University Press, 1956).
4. It has been suggested that it may also have been in Kirkcaldy that Smith found that the nailers received their wages in nails and used these nails afterwards as a currency in making purchases from the shopkeepers.
5. Quoted in John Rae, *Life of Adam Smith* (1895), p. 3.
6. For these and other details of Smith's schooling, see Fay, *op. cit.*

CHAPTER 3

1. Rae, *op. cit.*, pp. 12-13.

CHAPTER 4

1. Included in *Essays on Philosophical Subjects by the late Adam Smith*, 1795.
2. Scott, *op. cit.*, pp. 48-49.
3. But we shall later examine (see Chapter 5 below) evidence from a student's notes first published in 1963.
4. Quoted in W. R. Scott, *op. cit.*, pp. 51-52.
5. Printed in Scott, *op. cit.*, p. 379.

6. *Letters to Sir John Sinclair* (1791), p. 359. Quoted in C. R. Fay, *op. cit.*, p. 20.

7. W. R. Scott, *op. cit.*

CHAPTER 5

1. *Lectures on Rhetoric and Belles Lettres, Delivered in the University of Glasgow by Adam Smith*, edited with an Introduction and Notes by John M. Lothian (Thomas Nelson, 1963), p. 51.

2. *Ibid.*, p. 1.

3. *Ibid.*, p. 51.

4. *Ibid.*, p. 85.

5. *Ibid.*, p. 87.

CHAPTER 6

1. *Lectures on Policy, Justice, Revenue and Arms by Adam Smith*, edited by Edwin Cannan (Oxford: Clarendon Press, 1896), pp. 11 and 12. This will be referred to below as "Lectures."

2. Smith, however, made an exception with regard to patents and copyrights.

CHAPTER 7

1. F. H. Knight, *The Ethics of Competition* (Allen and Unwin, 1951), p. 23. The favorable effect of unfolding demands upon economic growth, i.e., their root connection with the nature and causes of the wealth of nations, is still more evident in Smith's *The Theory of Moral Sentiments*, chapter VIII, published in 1759. See also Nathan Rosenberg, "Adam Smith, Consumer Tastes, and Economic Growth," *The Journal of Political Economy*, June, 1968, pp. 361-374, and E. G. West, "Adam Smith's Philosophy of Riches," *Philosophy*, April, 1969.

2. *The Theory of Moral Sentiments*, 1759 (London: G. Bell and Sons, 1911), p. 339. This edition will be the subject of all further references.

CHAPTER 8

1. *Marx-Engels Gesamtansgabe* (Berlin, 1932), p. 536 .

2. *Ibid.*, p. 130.

3. *The Theory of Moral Sentiments*, p. 10.

4. See O. H. Taylor, *A History of Economic Thought* (McGraw-Hill, 1960), pp. 74-75.

5. Karl Marx, *Capital* (Everyman's Library, 1962), p. 654.

6. Some writers have argued that Smith recognized that some "excesses" of the division of labor caused alienation. It is true that he complained (in Book V of *The Wealth of Nations*) of the culturally restrictive effects of certain factory environments. However, this led him to suggest the provision of an antidote (education), not the later Marxian "cure": the abolition of capitalism. Smith, it will be remembered, tells us in the Glasgow lectures, "Opulence and Commerce commonly precede the improvement of arts and refinement of every sort." The division of labor in turn was his principal instrument for obtaining opulence and was thus indispensable. For a full examination of the contrasts between Smith and Marx on this subject see E. G. West, "Political Economy and Alienation: Karl Marx and Adam Smith," *Oxford Economic Papers* (March, 1969).

7. *The Theory of Moral Sentiments*.

8. Whatever may be the case in the next world, it is difficult to deduce from Smith's various instruments of "providential design" any certain harmony in this—even in the *Moral Sentiments*. Many of these instruments are destructive as well as constructive. Thus, while the love of machines may be a "necessary deception" to produce riches, it is an unnecessary deception when manifested in the desire of planners (lovers of system) to run society like their own clockwork. For further details of this ambiguity see E. G. West, "Adam Smith's Philosophy of Riches," *Philosophy*, March-April, 1969.

9. J. M. Buchanan, "Politics and Science: Reflections on Knight's Critique of Polanyi," *Ethics*, Vol. 77, No. 4 (July, 1967).

10. *Ibid.*

11. A. L. Macfie, *The Individual in Society: Papers on Adam Smith* (1967), Chapter 6.

12. *The Theory of Moral Sentiments*, p. 346.

13. This whole argument is contained in *The Theory of Moral Sentiments* in the opening three paragraphs of Part II, Section II, Chapter III.

14. *Ibid.* For an interesting discussion of Smith's distinction between

Beneficence and Justice see William F. Campbell, "Adam Smith's
Theory of Justice, Prudence and Beneficence," *American Economic Review*, Vol. LVII (May, 1967), p. 571.

15. J. M. Buchanan and Gordon Tullock in their *Calculus of Consent*
(1962) have developed in much stimulating detail this strand of
Smithian thought.

16. J. M. Buchanan (see footnote 9 above).

CHAPTER 9

1. Afterwards the Earl of Shelburne, the statesman.
2. Dugald Stewart, *Works* (Sir William Hamilton, Editor, Edinburgh, 1858), p. xvii.
3. *The Wealth of Nations*, Volume II, pp. 418-419.
4. Quoted in Rae, *op. cit.*, p. 57.
5. *The Correspondence of James Boswell and John Johnston of
Grange*, edited by Ralph S. Walker (London: Heinemann,
1966), p. 7. The quotation is reproduced here exactly as Boswell
spelled it.
6. Rae, *op. cit.*, p. 96.
7. Rae, *op. cit.*, p. 109.
8. Rae, *op. cit.*, pp. 110-111.
9. S. G. Checkland, *Scottish Journal of Political Economy* (February, 1967), pp. 75-76.
10. *Ibid.*, p. 77.
11. John Strang, *Glasgow and Its Clubs* (Glasgow, 1857), pp. 35-37.
12. S. G. Checkland, *op. cit.*, p. 79.

CHAPTER 10

1. Quoted in Rae, *op. cit.*, p. 205.
2. *Journal of Political Economy*, February, 1967, p. 106.
3. Quoted in Rae, *op cit.*, p. 215.
4. Rae, *op. cit.*, p. 369.
5. Frederick A. Pottle, *James Boswell* (Heinemann, 1966), p. 42.

CHAPTER 11

1. C. R. Fay, *Adam Smith* (Cambridge University Press, 1956),
p. 115.

2. C. R. Fay, *op. cit.*, p. 117.

CHAPTER 12

1. An interesting parallel is to be found in the argument of Milton Friedman in his *Capitalism and Freedom* (The University of Chicago Press, 1962). The discussion, which is supremely in the Smithian spirit, is cast in the modern American setting and deals with the predominance of the American Medical Association.

CHAPTER 13

1. See "Adam Smith's Rejection of Hume's Price-Specie-Flow Mechanism: A Minor Mystery Resolved," by Frank Petrella, *Southern Economic Journal*, Vol. XXXIV, No. 3 (January, 1968).
2. The most up-to-date summary of the debate between the new and the old orthodoxy on the question of the burden of the indirect debt is contained in *Public Debt and Future Generations*, edited by James M. Ferguson (The University of North Carolina Press, 1964).
3. Walter Bagehot, *Economic Studies* (London, 1880), p. 133.
4. F. A. Hayek, *The Confusion of Language and Thought*, Institute of Economic Affairs Occasional Paper 20 (London, 1968), p. 12.

CHAPTER 14

1. See M. A. Macfie, *The Economic Journal*, 1961, p. 151.
2. Both the letter and the account are in the Adam Smith museum at Kirkcaldy. I have not seen them reproduced elsewhere.
3. Rae, *op. cit.*, p. 346.

CHAPTER 15

1. Rae, *op. cit.*, pp. 331-332.

Bibliography

The best account of Adam Smith's life by a contemporary is to be found in Dugald Stewart's *Memoir* which was read to the Royal Society of Edinburgh in 1793 and is reproduced in Dugald Stewart's *Works*, Sir William Hamilton, Editor, Edinburgh, 1858. The principal biography, however, still remains John Rae's *Life of Adam Smith*, 1895. A new edition of this work was published with a special introduction by Professor Jacob Viner in 1965. Viner's introduction is an invaluable, up-to-date and exhaustive assessment of most of the topics of biographical interest that have been treated by specialists down to the mid-1960's. Another enlightening and informative piece of work is *Adam Smith and the Scotland of his Day*, by C. R. Fay, 1956. References on special aspects of Smith's life or writings are contained in the footnotes to each chapter of the present work. The best available version of *The Wealth of Nations* is the edition by Edwin Cannan, 1950. Apart from this there is Smith's eloquent, sensitive and illuminating *The Theory of Moral Sentiments*, 1759, a work which has received special attention in the present volume and to which all readers are most sincerely recommended.

The University of Glasgow's Bicentenary publications of all the known works and correspondence of Adam Smith began appearing from about 1969 onwards. All these publications will be re-edited. There will also appear in print for the first time a recently found manuscript set of notes of Smith's *Lectures on Jurisprudence* taken by a different student than the 1896 Edwin Cannan discovery. The new find apparently contains much more detail than the earlier one. In addition there will be appearing under the same auspices a volume of critical essays edited by T. Wilson of Glasgow University and a new biography by E. C. Mossner of the University of Texas.

For a stimulating and up-to-date economic assessment together with a succinct review of Smith's *The Wealth of Nations*, see M. Blaug, *Economic Theory in Retrospect* (second edition), Heinemann, London, 1968, chapter 2. *Adam Smith, 1776-1926*, first published in 1928 at the University of Chicago, contains an analysis by Paul Douglas of Smith's theory of value. Included in the same work is the famous essay by Jacob Viner, "Adam Smith and Laissez Faire." The piece by Douglas should be compared with the subsequent work of H. M. Robertson and W. L. Taylor, "Adam Smith's Approach to the Theory of Value," *Economic Journal*, 1957; D. F. Gordon, "What Was the Labour Theory of Value?", *American Economic Review*, May, 1959; and M. Blaug, "Welfare Indices in *The Wealth of Nations*," *Southern Economic Journal*, 1959. A reading of Viner's essay should be followed by a look at subsequent critical discussion of it by A. L. MacFie, *The Individual in Society* (University of Glasgow), 1967, chapter 6, and R. L. Crouch, "Laissez-Faire in Nineteenth Century Britain: Myth or Reality?," *Manchester School*, September, 1967. See also L. Robbins, *The Theory of Economic Policy*, 1952, Lectures I-III.

For an account of Smith's views on education see E. G. West, *Education and the State* (Institute of Economic Affairs, London, 1965), chapter 8, and "Private versus Public Education—A Classical Economic Dispute," *Journal of Political Economy*, October, 1964. On the Marxist interpretation of Smith's theory of value see R. L. Meek, *Studies in the Labour Theory of Value* (1956), chapter 2. The Marxist view is countered in Schumpeter, *History of Economic Analysis*, pp. 181-94. Adam Smith's sociology is outlined in *The Scottish Moralists*, edited and with an Introduction by Louis Schneider, 1967 (University of Chicago); A. Solomon, "Adam Smith as Sociologist," *Social Research*, February, 1954; and A. L. MacFie (*op. cit.*). For a general argument to the effect that Marxian sociology shows an affinity with Adam Smith's see R. L. Meek, *Economics and Ideology and Other Essays*, 1967, pp. 34-50, and Nathan Rosenberg, "Adam Smith on the Division of Labour: Two Views or One?", *Economica*, May, 1965. For counter arguments see E. G. West, "Adam Smith's Two Views on the Division of Labour," *Economica*, February, 1964, and "The Political Economy of Alienation in Karl Marx and Adam Smith," *Oxford Economic Papers*, March, 1969. In his *Polity and Economy*, 1957, Joseph Cropsey attempts to make a determinist psychological interpretation of *The Wealth of Nations* and *The Theory of Moral Sentiments*. For a reply see MacFie, *op. cit.*

On the historical, social, economic and intellectual background to Smith's writings see: R. Koebner, "Adam Smith and the Industrial Revolution," *Economic History Review*, April, 1959; A. Skinner, "Economics and History—The Scottish Enlightenment," *Scottish Journal of Political Economy*, February, 1965, and "Natural History in the Age of Adam Smith," *Political Studies*, 1967, Vol. XV, No. 1; C. B. A. Behrens, *The Ancien Regime*, 1967; T. S. Ashton, *An Economic History of England: The Eighteenth Century*, 1955; S. G. Checkland, "Adam Smith and the

Biographer," *Scottish Journal of Political Economy*, February, 1967.

Finally, there is James L. Clifford (editor), *Man Versus Society in Eighteenth Century Britain*, 1968—especially Chapter 2, "Man's Economic Status," by Jacob Viner; Nathan Rosenberg, "Adam Smith, Consumer Tastes, and Economic Growth," *The Journal of Political Economy*, June, 1968, pp. 361-374; E. G. West, "Adam Smith's Philosophy of Riches," *Philosophy*, April, 1969; and Frank Petrella, "Adam Smith's Rejection of Hume's Price-Specie-Flow Mechanism: A Minor Mystery Resolved," *Southern Economic Journal*, January, 1968.

NAME INDEX

SUBJECT INDEX